William Eleroy Curtis

Children of the Sun

William Eleroy Curtis

Children of the Sun

ISBN/EAN: 9783744753876

Printed in Europe, USA, Canada, Australia, Japan

Cover: Foto ©ninafisch / pixelio.de

More available books at **www.hansebooks.com**

The·Inter·Ocean

IS NOW PUBLISHED
EVERY DAY
IN THE YEAR.

Daily (including Sunday) per year, - - $12.00
Daily (excluding Sunday) per year, - - - 10.00
Wednesday's Edition (with Musical Supplement)
   per year - - - - - - - - 2.00
Saturday's Edition (sixteen pages) per year, - 2.00
Sunday's Edition (sixteen pages) per year, - - 2.00
Semi-Weekly Edition (published Monday and
   Thursday) per year, - - - - - 2.0
Weekly Edttion, per year, - - - - - 1.15

   Postage prepaid in each case.
   Sample copies sent on application.
   Remittances may be made at our risk either by draft, express, post office order, or registered letter. Money sent in any other way is at the risk of the person sending it. Address

THE INTER OCEAN,
85 MADISON ST., CHICAGO.

AMONG OTHER ATTRACTIONS offered the readers of the CHICAGO DAILY NEWS during 1883 will be a series of letters upon

THE ZUNIS,

THEIR TRADITIONS, FOLK-LORE, ANTIQUITIES, GOVERNMENT, SOCIOLOGY, ETC.,

FROM THE PEN OF

FRANK H. CUSHING.

Mr. Cushing has never before written for the Daily Press, and our contract with him gives us the exclusive right to publish his articles. It is his intention to so write them, that after their publication in the columns of the DAILY NEWS he will reprint in book form. This work will embrace all he has learned of the strange people during his sojourn in their pueblo.

THE CHICAGO DAILY NEWS is sold by Newsdealers everywhere. Price, 2 cents. By mail, $6.00 per year, or $1.00 for two months, postpaid.

NOW OPEN!
THE
CHICAGO & ATLANTIC
RAILWAY.

Trains leave South Side Union Depot, Cor. Polk Street and Fourth Avenue,

8.55 A. M. & 5.15 P. M.

FOR THE EAST.

The Equipment of this Company is the Most Elegant ever Built, and is from the Celebrated Pullman Company.

THE 5.15 P. M. TRAIN

RUNS THROUGH FROM

Chicago to New York Complete

Also a new Pullman Sleeping Car for Boston,

VIA ERIE RAILWAY

And All Classes of Passengers have Through Cars.

City Ticket Office, 119 Washington Street,

J. CONDIT SMITH,   S. W. SNOW,
Vice Pres't and Gen'l Manager.   Gen'l Passenger Agent.

CHICAGO.

The Great Rock Island Route

Still leads and is the favorite route to the ancient home of the
CHILDREN OF THE SUN.

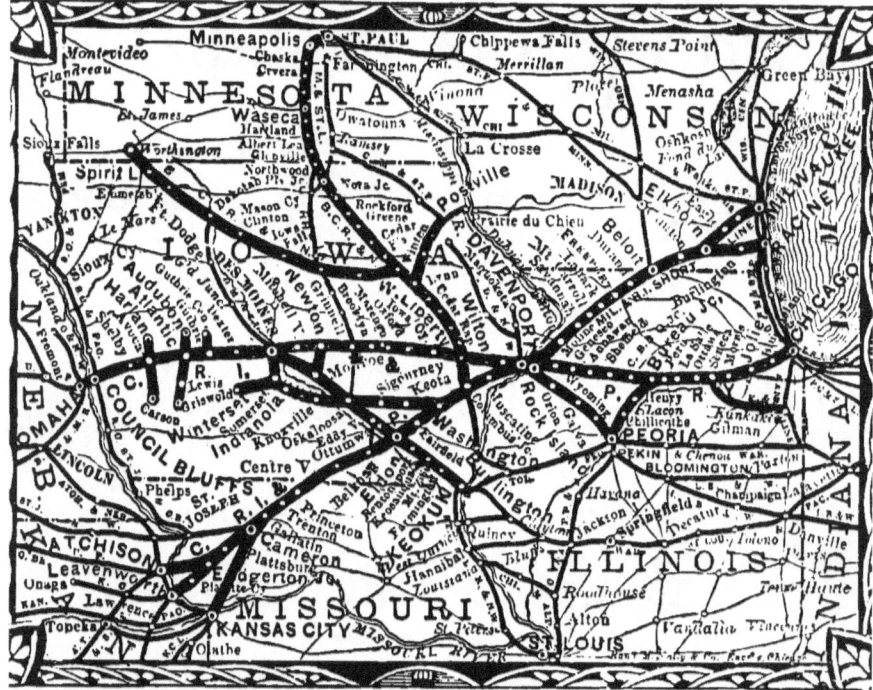

TWO EXPRESS TRAINS Leave CHICAGO Daily, for **KANSAS CITY, LEAVENWORTH** and **ATCHISON**, connecting with all the lines of railroad that penetrate **KANSAS, ARIZONA, COLORADO, NEW MEXICO** and **CALIFORNIA**. Also **TWO TRAINS** Daily to **COUNCIL BLUFFS**, and the same number by the famous

Albert Lea Route,
TO MINNEAPOLIS & ST. PAUL.

Parlor Reclining Chair Cars on all trains to Kansas City, and Pullman Palace Sleeping Cars, magnificent Day Cars and famous Dining Cars on Through Express Trains to all points.

R. R. CABLE,
Pres't and Gen'l Manager.

E. ST. JOHN,
Gen'l Ticket and Pass. Agt.

Children of the Sun.

BY WILLIAM E. CURTIS.

CHICAGO:
THE INTER-OCEAN PUBLISHING CO
1883.

COPYRIGHTED BY
WILLIAM E. CURTIS.

PRINTED BY
CLARK, PERRY & Co.,
CHICAGO.

CONTENTS.

I. A Visit to Our Oldest Inhabitants.

II. Mr. and Mrs. Cushing at Home.

III. A Senatorial Episode.

IV. Some Strange Coincidences and Curious Customs.

V. Zuni Religion and the Pilgrimage to the Sea.

VI. The Search for the Seven Cities of Gold.

VII. Queer People in Queer Places.

VIII. The Grand Canon of the Colorado and its Explorers

Children of the Sun.

CHAPTER I.

A VISIT TO A PECULIAR PEOPLE.

FAR to the Southwest, in the Sierra Madre range of the Rocky Mountains, just beyond the crest of "the grand Continental Divide," which forms the spinal column of the North American continent, in the midst of the thirsty desert, eight thousand feet above the level of the sea, is a little town, inhabited by a curious people who have furnished an interesting problem for ethnologists during the last three centuries, and are now attracting more attention than ever before. At the time of the conquest of Cortez it was called Cibola, meaning the city of the buffalo, but on the maps of to-day it appears as Zuni.

Amazing stories were told of the wealth and grandeur of its people—stories that excited the avarice of the whole empire of Spain, and drew upon them the assaults of a mighty army, excited by prospects of plunder, compared to which the hoarded gold and the silver-crested temples of the Montezumas were the merest trifle. At one time an army of fourteen thousand men, composed of the Spanish invaders and their Aztec allies, and led by a plumed Castillian, marched to its overthrow; but the dusty deserts and the impassable mountains discouraged and disheartened them, and a wise reconsideration of the plans of the viceroy saved the army from starvation in a land which afforded them no sustenance.

A second army followed ten years after, and conquered Zuni; but when it was found to be only a collection of mud huts the Spaniards destroyed the town, drove its inhabitants into the caves and cliffs of the mountains, and left it in disgust, seeking plunder elsewhere which they never found. For three and a half centuries Zuni slumbered, being disturbed only occasionally by a slight scientific survey, and escaping the eye of the world until the summer of 1882, when a party of its priests, under the guidance of Mr. Frank H. Cushing, went across the continent to Boston to fill their sacred gourds with water from "the ocean of the Sunrise," as their fathers had filled them from "the ocean of the Sunset" centuries ago. The debut of the Zuni upon the dramatic stage, for he is nothing if not dramatic, drew much attention to him of whom little was known before, and the eye of the scientific world is now fixed upon his curious customs, in the expectant hope of detecting in him a connecting link to an unknown, but much studied, prehistoric past. Without written language, knowing no English, and only enough Spanish for the purposes of trade, they have remained undisturbed in their primitive condition, and have not exhausted their old ideas or lost their ancient customs. Even the costume of the women is the same as that described by Coronado in 1541, and a place where fashions of dress do not change in more than three centuries would afford a fruitful study for the antiquarian, without taking into mind the curious myths and romantic traditions that afford an unprecedented field for ethnologists and poets.

Taking that wonderfully interesting railroad, the Atchison, Topeka and Santa Fe, to Albuquerque, then the new trans-continental line, the Atlantic and Pacific, we entered the mountains of Western New Mexico, and stopped at a station called Wingate, very near the Arizona boundary line. We found no town there; only a station-house and a water-tank, a young boy seated at a telegraphic instrument, and a great Newfoundland dog sleeping at his side. The boy said he was from Mount Vernon, Ohio, had been at that lonely mountain top all winter, and liked it. The dog could not talk, but had a history. He was found nearly starved by some track-builders a few months before in a snowdrift beside the body of a dead man, and the telegraph operator adopted him.

Three or four miles beyond this, under the shadow of a great mountain, stands Fort Wingate, one of the largest and most important military posts in the Southwest. The commandant is General Luther P. Bradley, who lived in Chicago before the rebellion, and went into the army at the head of the Fifty-first Illinois Regiment of Volunteers. He won the stars of a Brigadier General at the battle of Chickamauga, and when the war was over was made Colonel of the Thirteenth Regular Infantry, which he still commands. From Fort Wingate to Zuni the road follows an old trail over the rugged range of Zuni Mountains, from the summit of which can be had a grand view of the scenery for which Western New Mexico and Arizona are so famous. That picturesque and remarkable break of nature, the Navajo Church, looms up between the cliffs in the glory of its grandeur. It is not a church, however, but a massive rock, with two great shafts rising from it to the height of several hundred feet, like the spires of a cathedral. It is one of the most picturesque and unique effects of nature's sculpture, and is familiar to those who have had the opportunity of studying the photographs government explorers have made in this locality.

After riding for several hours over the mountains we came to the crest of a tremendous hill, nearly eleven thousand feet above the sea, and so steep as to be impassable for anything but a sure-footed mule or a mountain goat. The driver said he "would rather eat a six-shooter loaded and cocked than go down that hill with an ordinary wagon;" but the wheels were locked with chains, and the ambulance slid through the soft shale as if it had been snow instead of powdered slate.

Far off to the southward, where the blue of the sky and the gray of the earth blend in the haze, stretches a valley, narrow and crooked, closely embraced by picturesque mountains whose cliffs are cut in grotesque shapes. It is not entirely a charming region, this valley of the Zunis, but it is as remarkable in its peculiar attractions as are the peaceful heathen who within it dwell. Much is the rugged mountain, much is the water-worn cliff of clay, much is the dusty desert, much is the drifting sand, and much is the arid alkaline plain covered with the modest but nutritious gramma grass, and the wild sage, the wretchedest, most contemptible plant that grows.

It may be a grim and listless desert; it may be unbroken and undisturbed by glimpses of beauty, but the Zunis have lived here contented for centuries, and until lately thought there was no better land. They have plowed the dry soil with crooked sticks like the Egyptians used in the time of

Joseph, and watered it by digging ditches from the springs; they have planted their curious pink and yellow corn, and watched their grazing herds of sheep and cows and burros upon this dreary and desolate waste for centuries, and the bones of the generation who came here first lie in the inhospitable ground as dead as the dust of Adam; but a more contented, satisfied people were never seen. They have cures for the woes that ail them, and when no cure can apply they see in the failure the grim hand of fate, and lie down with a submission that is as sublime as Christian resignation. The Zunis are fatalists. They live only for their religion and to preserve their religious orders, and they believe that to die as Zunis should die is the great aim of life.

Sweet and soft around us was the spring air, melting toward sunset into a haze that seemed to fall like a veil of gauzy gold and hang between the blue mountains and the bluer sky. The sky seems bluer and wider and farther off here than anywhere else in the world, and we do not wonder in the grim and desolate silence that the Zunis love their land. The glowing dawns and the ruddy twilights, the vague summits of the far-off mountains covered with eternal snows, and the nearer mesa lines capped with grotesque shapes, eroded sandstone and clays that have been carved by the patient wind and rain into forms that are now as beautiful as the most shapely architecture, and again as preposterous as the crazy dreams of goblins; the fierce sun by day and the lazy moon and lambent stars by night, in a sky that scarcely ever knows a cloud—all these challenge the admiration of this little nation of savages, whose conversation is a poem, and whose traditions and legends are epics that compare with the choicest gems of Greece.

Farther down the beautiful valley of Las Nutrias (the Beavers), following a creek that comes from a great pool in the rocks, we reach a monstrous crag jutting out from the side of a mountain—the sacred Ta-ai-ia-lo-ne, where the Zunis believe the thunder resides—through which there is a venerable hole, 300 feet from the ground, elliptical in form, and large enough for an elephant to pass through without disturbing his plumage, if an elephant should be so foolish as to fly. Under the crag, on the ground, a shaft of stone, narrow and feather-shaped, stands upright sixty or seventy feet, where it fell when the knife of nature severed it from its sister crags.

The Zunis have a legend about this, as they have about every geological curiosity or absurdity, and the legend, as the old priests tell it, is this: Centuries ago the god of turquois—the Zunis believe every treasure sprang from the gods—had a wife who was the goddess of salt. To him they owe the rough, blue jewels that lie strewn upon their rocks, and to her the pitiless alkali that has eaten the vegetation off their plains. Indignant at the encroachments of the mortals, they flew away from their home, and in their flight the goddess dashed through the rock, which was resistless. One of her plumes was disarranged by the encounter and fell to the earth, the quill entering the ground. It stood upright, and turned to stone. Wherever she flew the ground was strewn with salt, and the vegetation destroyed, and the line of her flight is traced by beds of alkali that stretch to the Salt Lakes, where she rested forever. The Moquis and other Indians concede the ownership of these lakes to the Zunis, and have always paid them tribute for the privilege of gathering salt there, which has brought quite a revenue to the tribe.

The town of Zuni is a collection of mud huts, one above the other, until the highest is seven stories from the ground, and at the last census they numbered 1,602 people. The houses are built of adobe bricks—sun-dried clay—and the walls of the lower strata of rooms are, in in some cases, seven and eight feet thick. These are roofed over with the trunks of cottonwood and pine trees, covered with a thick layer of straw and clay. The walls of one house are the foundation of another, and the roof of one is the floor of that which stands above it. The houses as a usual thing are entered from the roof, and the interior is reached by climbing a ladder up and then climbing a ladder down. This mode of construction was adopted as a measure of protection from the assaults of outside enemies, and when a Zuni wants to lock his dwelling he pulls up the ladder. It is the old story of the woodchuck that went into his hole and pulled the hole in after him. In the center of the town is a wide court, or plaza, which is reached by climbing seven ladders to the top of the pueblo, and then climbing down seven more to the ground. In this court are held the councils and sacred dances, which Mr. Cushing has described in such a graphic way in his contributions to the *Century.*

We were stretched around upon the soft sheepskins, listening with absorbing interest to the recital of Mr. Cushing's peculiar adventures, when the Governor, Pa-lo-wah-ti-wah, came in. By the brilliant light that came from the blazing branches of the piñon tree which flamed in the rude but picturesque corner fireplace, we could see a tall, gaunt man, with large, dark eyes, a sharp nose and a melancholy mouth—an Indian counterpart in countenance of Edwin Booth.

"Here is the old Governor come to call upon you," said Mr. Cushing, and we arose and were introduced to him as "men who make meaning marks—friends of mine from Chicago."

The old savage grasped my hand, drew it to his mouth, and breathed upon it. That is the friendly salutation of the Zuni—a beautiful one in its significance, for it meant that he gave his breath, the most precious gift that he had, into my hand.

"May you grow to be a tall man," was his salutation in Zuni to me, referring to my inferior stature.

The Governor squatted down on a sheepskin rug, and I offered him a cigar. He took it with a profound bow of thanks, and lit it with an ember that he lifted from the fireplace. Pretty soon, after he had pulled a few whiffs, he jumped up, ran to the door and threw away the cigar, apologizing for lighting it in the presence of ladies, and teaching us a lesson in politeness. He was assured that the ladies had been well cured, being the wives of inveterate smokers, and accepting another cigar, puffed away with the rest of us.

With Mr. Cushing as interpreter, we talked with him, and he expressed the admiration he felt for the greatness of Chicago. It was the first large city he saw on his Eastern trip, in the summer of 1882, and his recollections were amusing and interesting. While they were there the Zunis stopped at the Palmer House, the biggest pueblo he was ever in, and witnessed an American dance in the ballroom. He laughed heartily as he told of some of his party who tried to dance and slipped down upon the waxed floor, but solemnly assured us that he had been guilty of no such foolishness. The Governor's costume was unique, if not impressive. He wore a shirt and pair of drawers made of flour sacks, and across his shoulder-blades was printed the legend, in large blue letters, " XXX Superfine Winter Wheat Patent Flour," and the name of the miller, which his Excellency considered a great ornament. He was glad to see us as the friends of his brother, "Te-nah-tsa-li"—" Medicine Flower," as the Zunis have named Cushing, and, in his Oriental way, wished that our visit " might be blessed with a multitude of pleasures."

The Governor has been Mr. Cushing's steadfast friend through many a crisis, and adopted him as his "brother" when he first came to Zuni. He has been Cushing's teacher during his study of the language, and has proved an affectionate and wise counsellor. His badge of office is an old ivory headed cane—the same insignia is found in all the New Mexican Pueblos, and is suspended by a faded red ribbon which came around some papers sent to the tribe by President Lincoln. When Cushing came to Zuni he found a home in the Governor's house, and in one of his articles for *The Century*, thus describes the family :

" The family consisted of the governor's ugly wife, a short-statured, large-mouthed, slant-eyed, bushy-haired hypochondriac, yet the soul of obedience to her husband, and ultimately of kindness to me, for she conceived a violent fancy for me, because I petted her noisy, dirty, and adored little niece. Not so was her old aunt, a fine-looking, straight little old woman of sixty winters, which had bleached her abundant hair as white as snow. The Governor did not love her. He called her 'Old Ten,' which, as he explained, referred to the number of men she had jilted, and which appellation unloosed a tongue that the Governor avowed 'knew how to talk smarting words.' Then there was the Governor's brother-in-law, a short, rather thick and greasy man, excessively conceited, ignorant, narrow, and moreover, so ceaselessly talkative, that he merited the name the inventive and sarcastic chief had given him, 'Who-talks-himself-dry.'"

"If the governor loved not 'Old Ten,' he despised her favorite nephew. This fellow's wife, however, was good-looking, dignified, quiet, modest, and altogether one of the most even-tempered women, red or white, it has been my lot to know. She was always busy with her children, or with the meal-grinding and cookery, occasionally varying these duties with belt-making or weaving. The little niece and her older brother were the only children. The former was a little child, rather too small for her age. She was the small 'head of the household.' All matters, however important, had to be calculated with reference to her. If she slept, the household duties had to be performed on tiptoe, or suspended. If she woke and howled, the mother or aunt would have to hold her, while 'Old Ten' procured something bright-colored and waved it frantically before her. If she spoke, the whole family must be silent as the tomb, or else bear the indignation of three women and one man. The governor despised the father too much to join in this family worship. Indeed, while the rest delighted in speaking of this short specimen of humanity by the womanly name of 'Iu-i-si-a-wih-si-wih-ti-tsa,' the Governor called her a 'bag of hard howls,' and said that she had the habit of storing up breath like a horned toad, which accounted for her extraordinary circumference, and her ability to make a noise in the world.

"Little Iu-ni, her brother, was as handsome and as nearly like his mother as boy could be, save that he was rather inconsiderate to dumb things, and to his little sister's hideous dolls.

"The aged grandfather of this group was usually absent after wood, or else puttering near the fire-place, or on the sunny terrace. He was lean as Disease, and black as his daughter—which expressed a good deal to her husband, the Governor,—with toothless under-jaw and weeping eyes. The Navajos had treated him roughly in his youth, which he showed by the odd mixture of limp, shuffle, and jump in his gait. The asthma had tried for years to kill him; but he only coughed and wheezed harder and harder, as winter succeeded winter. So explained his son-in-law, the Governor, who, if he ever mentioned him at all, called him 'the Ancient Hummer.'"

Pretty soon there was a timid rap at the door—a custom Mrs. Cushing has introduced. The Zunis enter the houses of each other without ceremony, at all times of day and night, not even asking as much as by your leave—but Mrs. Cushing has forbidden them to intrude into her apartments without permission, and since she has made frightful examples of some of them, they have adopted the civilized mode of knocking at the door and awaiting a welcome.

When Cushing cried out in Zuni "come in," the door slowly opened, and there appeared a fat little woman who stepped to the table and emptied from her blanket a large quantity of parched corn, explaining that she had prepared it for the friends of "Cushy-Cushy," as the scientist is more familiarly known. She intimated that some compensation would be acceptable, and was rewarded by the ladies of the party who offered her a few pieces of candy they had brought with them. To this Mrs. Cushing objected, as the knowledge that sweetmeats were in our possession would bring the whole community to the door; but the woman got her reward with an emphatic injunction that there was no more to be had.

When I asked the old Governor what he remembered most pleasantly of all he saw in Chicago, he referred to a big pueblo with beautifully colored walls, dazzling lights, and brilliant blankets hanging from gold and silver rods, which he visited with Mr. Cushing. He said that there was a young lady on the stage who sang and talked and danced, and he thought she was very beautiful and bright, and he liked her the best of any of the American ladies he saw on his journey East. Mr. Cushing explained that his Excellency referred to the Grand Opera House, of Chicago, and that the young lady whose attractions had left so profound an impression upon his soul was Miss Minnie Palmer, whom he saw in her play, "My Sweetheart." The Governor was also very much pleased and impressed with the comic opera "The Mascotte," which he witnessed on that memorable journey, and sang to us the "Gobble, Gobble, Baa!" ditty, which he distinctly remembered, and has been singing about Zuni ever since.

The people in the streets of Chicago, he said, "were so many that it gave him thoughts," meaning that they caused him a great deal of wonder and bewilderment.

The Governor had not long been gone before the presence of his worthy spouse was announced, and in she came to pay her respects to the ladies. She is short of stature, as all women of the Zunis are. They marry at ten years of age, and many of them are mothers at twelve, so that with the cares of the household they never get their growth. She had not an unpleasant face, but there was a sharp look in the eye and a curl of the lip that revealed her disposition as plainly as if it had been photographed on paper, and Mrs. Cushing said that our estimate of her characteristic was not a mistaken one, for she has the sharpest tongue in the village. She is a good woman, honest, neat and industrious, and not given to vanities; but a terrible scold and the worst gossip in the town. Her husband has for twenty years been aware of her proclivities, for she abuses him as if he were a scullery grubber instead of the chief magistrate of the tribe, and Mr. Cushing says that when he lived with them he was kept awake all night many a time by the Caudle lectures she delivered to the old gentleman as he reposed by her side upon their couch of sheepskin.

Her ladyship wore a sort of tunic made of the same material as her blanket, blue being the prevailing color, with here and there an irregular stripe of white. The shoulder bands were richly embroidered with beads, and the leggings were made to match. Upon her feet were a pair of handsome moccasins, and over her head she wore a well-bleached flour sack in the place of a hood or shawl. Her ornaments were quite conspicuous, and consisted of a heavy necklace of large silver beads, with a pendant in the form of a crescent, hammered out of a silver dollar by her devoted husband, who is quite a skillful silversmith. From her ears hung heavy ear-rings of silver, large and fantastic in shape, like those worn upon the opera stage by gypsy queens. Around her wrists were bracelets innumerable, all of silver, some of them engraved bands, and others strings of beads and buttons.

She dropped a courtesy as she entered the door, and said, apologetically, that her husband had told her to come and see the ladies, although she "was quite covered over with shame because she had been eating onions," not having expected company. Mrs. Cushing indulged in a sotto voce dissent from the remark that her visit had been at the suggestion of her husband, and ventured the assertion that the old gentleman had received a terrible blowing up because he had made his call before she had an opportunity. She breathed upon the ladies' hands as the Governor had breathed upon those of the gentlemen, and bade them welcome to the hospitable homes of Zuni. Some of the ornaments and garments the ladies wore seemed to arrest her attention, and she was particularly enchanted with a chatelaine watch which hung from the belt of one of them. Their fur-lined mantles she considered quite a luxury, and was outspoken in her admiration thereof. One of the mantles bore at the neck a silver-plated clasp, which seemed to suit her fancy, and was regarded by her as a gem of priceless value.

During her short call she proved the power of a woman's discerning eye by detecting which of the three ladies in our party was single and which were married, but congratulated them all in a most flattering way upon their beautiful appearance. As she left the room she bestowed upon us quite a polite and pretty blessing, when she said in Zuni:

"May the darkness bring sweet sleep to you all, and may the morning find you well."

Before going, however, she invited the ladies to return the call, and intimated that she had some very nice pottery of her own manufacture and decoration that she was willing to dispose of. It is unnecessary to say that the ladies accepted the invitation and bought the pottery.

During the evening we strolled about the village, looking in upon the people and seeing how they lived. Their rooms were lighted by pinons blazing in the fire-places, and the shadows were very picturesque. At one place the man we wanted to see was out, but we found a little woman crooning over a sick baby which lay naked in her arms, and giving it medicine from a bowl of steaming herbs that sat beside the fire. She was singing a song to put the child asleep and rocking it gently in her arms.

One of the wierdest pictures I ever witnessed was that presented at the house of the high-priest of the Pueblo, a venerable old man, Nai-iu-tchi by name. He was about retiring when we called, and the fire on the hearth was low. Retiring with the Zunis means pulling a lot of sheepskins into a corner and lying down upon them.

The old man recognized Cushing's voice and gave him an affectionate welcome. As we entered he arose from his couch and breathed into our hands one after another, uttering a poetic phrase about the gladness that came in with us at the open door. All the Zunis are poets, and there is nothing so conspicuous in their habits and customs and language as the striking resemblance to the oriental in their salutations and benedictions. He apologized for the darkness of the room, and called to his wife to "shake the flame out of the embers." She responded jestingly that he was getting old and lazy and "was no good any more," or he would get up and fix the fire himself. As the flames began to blaze out of the wood the light crept upon the shadows and showed us the recumbent forms of several of the family stretched out under their blankets peacefully snoring. The old priest sat cross-legged like a Turk in their midst, with his gray hair falling upon his shoulders, and the fitful shadows from the firelight playing around the wrinkles in his solemn, rugged face.

I did not see him by daylight, and the abbreviated garments he wore that night were not consonant with the dignity that sat upon his face; but the picture he made was an effective one. His head is large and leonine, and the abundant hair fell upon his shoulders like a mane; his face was cast in a heroic mold, and its features are those of a prophet. The incongruity between the head and the drapery could not have been more striking or comic. It was a bust of Plato in bronze draped in a pink calico shirt.

He, too, like the Governor, wanted to talk of Chicago; but, unlike that gay and giddy executive, the old priest took the wonders of civilization home to his poor untutored soul. He had nothing to say of the ball-room at the Palmer House, nor of the theater; but the advantages and benefits and blessings of civilization seemed to have impressed him most. While the Governor's observations had been those of "a man about town," the old priest had looked through the eyes of a philosopher. Only once did he drop from his tone of apostolic dignity, and that was when he alluded to the elephant Jumbo, which he said was the most wonderful animal he ever saw, and bigger than he supposed the gods created them. Then he added, gleefully:

"I have his picture in my little treasure box."

I asked him what of all he saw at Chicago gave him the most gratification, and to our surprise the venerable old priest said: "the sea lions at Lincoln Park!" Why? Because, as he piously explained, they were the first creatures carrying life in their breasts he had ever seen that came from the ocean, which the Zunis worship. Like other people they worship that which they deem most precious. With the Christian it is the water of life. With the Zunis it is the water of the sea, the river and the spring; that which alone stands between them and starvation in this parched and arid land. In the sea lions the old priest saw "the children of the ocean" for the first time, and his soul was filled with awe and reverence. When the party reached the fountain at Lincoln Park where the sea lions are kept, the old priest and his companions, ran up to the iron railing, exclaiming: "At last, at last, we greet thee; oh! our fathers!" And they began praying most fervently, at the same time sprinkling sacred meal upon the water.

I asked him then what was the most wonderful thing he saw in all his journey through civilization, and he answered, "The sleight-of-hand men." When they were in New York the Zunis went to see the jugglers, and to this day Cushing cannot convince them that they were not gods.

The contortionists at the circus were also considered supernatural by them. While at Boston they were taken to see the negro minstrels one night by the Mayor. At first they were enthusiastic over the clog-dancing and various other feats, and expressed themselves in peculiar shrill cries of approbation. But suddenly they became silent, for they conceived the idea that they were witnessing the mysterious rites of one of the religious orders of America, and they therefore repeatedly stretched out their arms to draw in the spirit of the "holy men" upon the stage.

But I was not satisfied with the old man's answers. I could not believe one with a face like that which the priest bore had looked no deeper than this into the triumphs of the pale faces. So I put this question:

"What of all you saw in your journey East impressed you most with the superiority of the white men over the Indians?"

The father of the Zunis turned his eyes towards me, and answered slowly: "The ease with which they can get water. The white man takes the river into the walls of his house. By turning a little iron stick he can get that which we pray for all our lives!"

This to the mind of the Zuni, the inhabitant of a barren, rainless land, was the triumph of civilization. I asked him if he wanted to go back to the States, and he said, "Yes; I grow strong with anxiety that I may go again."

CHAPTER II.

MR. AND MRS. CUSHING AT HOME.

UNTIL Mr. Cushing began to write his interesting descriptions of a peculiar people, the Zunis were almost entirely unknown, but they have been made famous by his researches and narrations, and by the publicity given to their journey to the sea. They are the oldest, as far as is known, and the least undisturbed in their primitive conditions of all the Indians in the United States; they have never received aid from the government, and therefore their name does not appear in the records at Washington, nor in the appropriation bills of Congress. Three or four hundred years ago a great deal was said of them in the reports of the old Spanish explorers, who invaded this country in their remorseless search for gold, but from Coronado, who wrote of them in 1550, to Cushing, who commenced to write of them two years ago, they have been allowed to live along in their primitive simplicity, nestled down among the mountains, off the line of travel, beyond the reach of ordinary scientists, and in a country that offers no quartz or gold dust as temptations to the ubiquitous prospector.

Mr. Cushing is a very young man, not more than twenty-four years of age, slight of physique, slender of stature, but of wonderful nerve, unusual intelligence and consuming ambition. His researches here and his contributions to literature have already given him fame as an ethnologist and an author. He came originally from Medina, N. Y., and in his youth had a remarkable *penchant* for antiquities. His first work in this line was an investigation of some of the old Indian mounds in Central New York, and it attracted the attention of the officers of the Smithsonian Institute, who gave him a position upon their staff. In 1879 when an expedition was about to leave for New Mexico, to explore among the mountains where the ancient Pueblos lie, and in the hills where the cliff-dwellers lived in the days we know nothing of, Prof. Baird directed him to accompany it. The instructions given the party were to find the most curious and primitive of these tribes—that one, wherever it was, of which science had the smallest knowledge, and which had felt the least the advance of civilization. At that place, and with that tribe, young Cushing was to remain, and spend as much time as necessary in the study of its language, customs and traditions. It was supposed that one season would be sufficient, and Cushing expected to return with the exploring party to Washington when winter came, but it was a case of miscalculation, for Cushing is at Zuni still, and expects to remain there for two or three years longer until he has reached the end of his researches, and reaped the most fruitful scientific harvest that ever was gathered by an ethnologist's hand.

I do not believe Mr. Cushing or any other scientist would have undertaken the work had he known what was before him; had he known what the penalty was, the obstacles that were to be encountered, the hardships that were to be endured, and the privations that were to be suffered, but having plunged in he had to stay. His experience has been one of unexampled novelty, but at the same time requiring more nerve and courage and endurance than even a scientific fanatic would often be willing to confront. And such words fitly describe Mr. Cushing. Those who are jealous of him say that he is doing all that he has done in order to secure notoriety. That he finds in his field an opportunity to gain a professional reputation beyond and above that which exists in other resorts of the ethnologists is no doubt true, but I do not believe a mere thirst for notoriety could have kept him here, when the bauble could be so easily found in other and less arduous fields. His work is the result of an inspiration accidentally received, and he is determined to be thorough.

No one can see or talk with Mr. Cushing without realizing that he is an enthusiast, helpless against the ambition that has become a passion for acquiring knowledge of this interesting and remarkable people, and those who visit the place, honestly and unprejudiced, will acknowledge that he is entitled to all the reputation, or notoriety, if that word will suit better, that will cling to his name. In demeanor he is modest but enthusiastic; in conversation, fascinatingly interesting, and a study of his writings about the Zunis will show a labored attempt to conceal his individualism so far as it can possibly be done. His articles would be more interesting if he would relate more of himself and his remarkable experience, for it is unique and unprecedented, and I know of no one who has undergone anything that can parallel his life for the last few years that would write of it so modestly and unostentatiously as he does. Having first read his publications, and then visited him at his home, I can see how much of absorbing interest might have been written, but never has been, and probably never will be told. He has impaired his health, and will be a dyspeptic for life, because of the effect upon his stomach of the fierce and vile concoctions which these Indians use for food, and he bears upon his person marks of heroism and martyrdom in the causes of science, than which there is no better evidences of his gaminess, his endurance, his courage and self-sacrifice. During our visit to Zuni the subject was not alluded to, as Mr. Cushing said he had very little time or disposition to talk about himself; and the stay there was so limited that our conversation was devoted almost entirely to the Indians, and not to him. But from other sources—from the officers at Fort Wingate, who know more about him and his work from their close observation during the entire period of his life at Zuni—we learned much of his experience and adventures.

As the Zunis are a secretive and suspicious people ; as their religious rites and ceremonies are all sacredly secret, and performed in the temples, or *estufas*, which no one but members of their secret orders are allowed to enter, Mr. Cushing found great difficulty and danger in pursuing his work.

In order to gain their confidence he adopted their costume, imitated their customs and habits, assisted them at their work, and ate their food. He submitted to all the tests they desired to apply to him, and with the Zunis, as with all other Indians, a man's worth is estimated by the degree of his nerve and endurance. The young men, before they can become warriors, are subjected to fearful tests to try their metal and their courage, and he who can endure the most is the greatest warrior, and is selected as the chief. To every student of Indian customs, to every one who is familiar with their modes of determining the courage of their men, it is enough to say that Mr. Cushing is the war-chief of the tribe and a member of the highest priesthood—the Sacred Order of the Bow. And he has attained these offices in three years' residence among them by showing that he has more endurance than the strongest, more nerve than the most stolid, and more courage than the bravest man amongst them. He voluntarily, in order to gain their confidence, offered to submit to any tests they might determine, and they took the offer for all it meant. There is no member of the tribe who has gone through so much as he, and the stuff that he is made of was the argument that advanced him in the chieftancy of the tribe.

But the worst of all, the most obnoxious and revolting experience of his entire stay among them, was the necessity of eating their food. The concoctions which they prepare of meat and herbs and garlic and peppers require a copper-lined and brass-riveted stomach to receive and digest. But he swallowed it without a protest, to the peril of his health, and the result is the ruin of his stomach and the poisoning of his blood. Mr. Cushing is a man of fair complexion, light hair and delicate stomach. For months he suffered intensely from indigestion after eating their mixtures that seem made of fire, and as a consequence a scrofulous tendency has developed into painful and disagreeable eruptions upon his face. Since he has secured their confidence and an influential position in the tribe he is permitted to prepare his own food, and he now does so, but finds himself as the result of his voluntary experience a chronic dyspeptic, with his blood full of poison, for which his brother, who is a physician, is now at Zuni giving him heroic treatment.

Is Cushing genuine? We asked everybody we saw around Wingate that question, and there was not one who had other than kind words for him, and strong expressions of faith in the fidelity and accuracy of his work. The missionary who visits the Zunis, the Indian agent who has the official oversight of the tribe, while each of them object to some features of Cushing's work, both deny the charge that he is an impostor, and testify to his truthfulness. Some of those with whom we talked do not, of course, enter into the spirit of Cushing's work, nor appreciate its value. Some of them called him a crank and a fool, as they would consider any one who would waste the best years of his life, and suffer hardships and privations for the cause of science. Others thought he was an enthusiast who saw in the Indian legends and traditions more poetry and romance than sober, practical utility; but they all vouched for his genuineness and honesty. In a private letter Mr. Cushing modestly describes the object of his life at Zuni, as follows:

"The purposes of my sojourn among these Indians have been to secure as much knowledge of their traditional history, mythology, sociologic organization, manners and customs,—religious as well as secular,—linguistics, arts and industries as possible. This data is designed for the reconstruction, not only of the Spanish and Aboriginal history of these parts, but also of material knowledge and better understanding of the "Indian Question," which the Government now deems of enough importance to require quite wide and special investigation.

"At the outset I was in a certain manner left dependent on the Indians, in consequence of which, and later, of a desire to overcome their conservatism and suspicion of my matters, I was compelled to adopt their manner of life, language and costume.

"Thus, and through other means I came to gain high position in their councils, a sub-chieftancy, the second chieftancy, and lastly—a position which I still and probably shall continue to occupy so long as I remain among them, Membership in the Medicine Order of Warriors, or "Priesthood of the Bow," and the Permanent Head War Chieftancy. I have, of course, been long ago adopted into their tribe, as have, from time to time, wards from among the Moquis, Pueblos and Navajos, and at present and for all time shall enjoy—so far as they are concerned—the full rights of *Gentile* or clanship nationality."

When he first arrived at Zuni the Indians tried to drive him away. Now they are absurdly jealous in their regard for him, and observe the attentions he receives from visitors there with mingled gratification and dislike. They are particularly anxious for him to remain with them during his entire life; and in all cases of difficulty, the threat that he will go back to "the Land of Day" brings them to terms. After he had been left in the village by the party of explorers the Indians drove him out, and even went so far as to threaten his life; but the Governor took him under his protection, and having conceived a fancy for the young paleface, adopted him as a brother, and admitted him to his own household. The first requirement made of him was to eat the food of the people, and adopt their dress.

Mr. Cushing's costume is very unique and becoming. While it would scarcely do in civilized society, because of its conspicuous unlikeness to anything worn in the present day, it is handsome and comfortable. He wears no hat, like all Zunis, but around the crown of his head is tied a black silk scarf, folded, the fringed ends of which hang down over his right ear. His upper garment is a blue blouse, such as the soldiers wear, embroidered upon the shoulders, at the waists and down the front with many silver buttons. Around his neck is a heavy necklace made of silver coin, hammered by the native silversmiths into curious shapes, and engraved with strange devices. Alternating with these medals are large stones of unpolished turquois, just as they were found among the rocks, except for the holes drilled through them. His belt is of buckskin, to which are attached large silver medals hammered from American dollars, with a handsomely embroidered knife sheath hanging on the left side, and on the right a long strap which trails upon the ground. This strap is loaded with silver buttons, and is used as a whip by the Zunis when riding to beat their mules and horses. Across his shoulder, like a sash, is a buckskin arrangement, with long fringe, handsome embroidery and innumerable silver buttons, which supports the quiver of arrows hanging upon his back. He wears knee-breeches, of blanket cloth, native woven, embroidered and fringed down the sides, with the usual rows of silver buttons. His garters are beautifully embroidered, and are woven in colors from the wool of the sheep. His stockings are black, also of native wool, and knit by the Indians, and when he is abroad he wears anklets of buckskin for protection against cactus and briars. On his feet are the usual moccasins.

When in full war dress, arrayed for the dance or religious ceremonials, he carries a beautiful bow and a shield made of horse hide, decorated with colors by skillful native artists, and heavily fringed with buckskin thongs, fastened to its edge by silver ornaments.

After he had adopted the dress of the tribe, his foster father and many other of the principal men of the tribe insisted that his ears should be pierced. "I steadily refused, writes Mr. Cushing, " but they persisted, until at last it occurred to me that there must be some meaning in their urgency, and I determined to yield to their request. They procured some raw Moqui cotton, which they twisted into rolls about as large as an ordinary lead-pencil. Then they brought a large bowl of clear cold water and placed it before a rug in the eastern part of the room. K'iawu presently came through the doorway, arrayed in her best dress, with a sacred cotton mantle thrown over her shoulders, and abundant white shell beads on her neck. I was placed kneeling on the rug, my face toward the east. My old father, then solemnly removing his moccasins, approached me, needle and cotton in hand. He began a little shuffling dance around me, in time to a prayer chant to the sun. At the pauses in the chant he would reach out and grasp gently the lobe of my left ear. Each time he grasped I braced up to endure the prick, until finally, when I least expected it, he ran the needle through. The chant was repeated, and the other ear grasped and pierced in the same way. As soon as the rolls of cotton had been drawn through, both the old man and K'iawu dipped their hands in the water, prayed over them, and, at the close of the prayer, sprinkled my head, and scattered the water about like raindrops on the floor; after which they washed my hands and face, and dried them with the cotton mantle.

"I could not understand the whole prayer, but it contained beautiful passages, recommending me to the gods as a "Child of the Sun," and a "Son of the Coru people of earth" (the sacred name for the priests of Zuni). At its close the old man said: "And thus become thou my son, Te-na-tsa-li" (Medicine Flower). And the old woman followed him with, "This day thou art made my younger brother, Te-na-tsa-li." Various other members of the little group then came forward, repeating the ceremonial and prayer, and closing with one or the other of the above sentences, and the distinct pronunciation of my new name.

"When all was over, my father took me to the window, and, looking down with a smile on his face, explained that I was 'named after a magical plant that grew on a single mountain in the West, the flowers of which were the most beautiful in the world, and of many colors, and the roots and juices of which were a panacea for all injuries to the flesh of man. That by this name,—which only one man in a generation could bear,—would I be known as long as the sun rose and set, and smiled on the Coru people of earth, as a *Shi wi* (Zuni).'"

At first Mr. Cushing's sketch book was an object of horror among the tribe. The art of drawing pictures was regarded as sorcery, and for the freedom with which he sketched their dances Mr. Cushing several times narrowly escaped with his life. Among his drawings was the portrait of a pretty little girl. An old white-headed grandmother, looking the sketches over one day, recognized this. She shook her head, frowned, and, covering her face with her withered hands, began to cry and howl most dolefully. At intervals during the remainder of the day he could hear her talking, scolding, and sobbing over what she regarded as a great misfortune to her family. But old Pedro Pino had seen photographs and other pictures among the soldiers, and one day, in remonstrating with one of the tribe whose face had been sketched to his disgust, he said: "Though your body perish, nevertheless you shall continue to live on upon the earth. Your face will not be forgotten now; though your hair turn gray, it will never turn gray here. I know this to be so, for I have seen, in the quarters of the officers at the fort, the faces of their fathers, who have long since passed from earth, but still were looking down upon their children from the wall."

On the journey to the East, Mr. Cushing exchanged his picturesque garb for the clothing of civilization when the party arrived at Fort Wingate. The question of his wearing "American clothes" on the trip had been a serious one with the Zunis, and it was a subject of many deliberations. Assent was given only on the representation that it would displease his brothers the Americans should he not do it, their feeling for conventionality in dress being as strong as that of the Zunis. This motive was one that appealed to them forcibly and was readily understood. He did not cut his hair, however, until the arrival at Chicago, as he did not desire to ask too much of them at one time. It was eighteen inches long, and made him disagreeably conspicuous. He told them that the American *Caciques* (priests) desired that it should be cut, and it would gratify his brothers the Americans, and show them that the Zunis were considerate of their wishes. The Zunis could not see how it was that the Americans objected to long hair, which was the crowning glory of a man. They were slow in consenting, and could only be persuaded by the promise of Mr. Cushing that he would have it made up, so that he could wear it beneath his head-band when at Zuni, "for," said they, "no one could become a member of the Ka-ka without long hair."

The Indians were very anxious for him to marry into the tribe, but this he positively declined to do. Twice were nut-brown maidens selected for him by his brother, and guardian, the Governor, and the latter was very much offended at their rejection. Mr. Cushing tells the story of the attempt to ensnare him into the matrimonial net as follows :

I had nearly given up seeing a pair of garters which had been promised me, when one day, all bustle and smiles, the "Little Mother" came in bearing them. They were beautiful and well made —they endure even yet—and with matronly pride she laid them before me. I paid her liberally, that the subject of Lai-iu-lut-sa should not be resumed. But it was broached by the Governor. That night, when we were alone, he came and lay down by my side where I was writing.

"Get a big piece of paper," said he, and, knowing him, I obeyed.

"Now write." I seized a pencil.

"'Thou comest?' said he, in his own language.

I wrote it and pronounced it.

"Good," said he; then added :

"'Yes; how are you these many days?'

"'Happy!' 'Sit down.' 'Eat.' (Then a tray of bread will be placed before you; but you must be polite, and eat but little, and soon say:) 'Thanks.'

"'Eat enough. You must have come thinking of something. What have you to say?'

"'I don't know.'

"'Oh! yes, you do; tell me.'

"'I'm thinking of you' (in a whisper).

"'Indeed! You must be mistaken.'

"'No!'

"'Aha! do you love me?'

"'Ay, I love you.'

"'Truly?'

"'Yes!'

"'Possibly; we will see. What think you, father?'

"'As you think, my child' (the father will say)."

"What in the name of the moon does all this mean, brother?" I asked him when he had read me the questions and answers over two or three times, and said I had pronounced them all right.

"It means what you will say to Lai-iu-lut-sa to-morrow night when you go to see her."

I was perplexed. I knew not what to say, as I feared offending the good old man.

"Look here, brother, I can't go to see her; she would laugh at me because I can't speak good Zuni yet."

"Now, that's all I have to say to you," he replied, angrily. "I've done my best for you; fools will be fools, not even their brothers can help it. I see you propose to live single and have everybody say: 'There goes a man that no woman will have; not even when his brother helps him.' No! Do you suppose I am blind? You are no Zuni; you want to go back to Washington; but you can't, I tell you. You might as well get married; you *are* a Zuni—do you hear me? You are a fool, too!"

With this he left me; nor would he speak to me again for many days, save on the most commonplace affairs of life, and then but briefly.

My old father here came to my relief. He persuaded the vexed Governor that perhaps Lai-iu-lut-sa did not suit me, and that my refusal of her was no argument against my love for her people. With a sublime sense of his power of diplomacy, he also sat down to have a talk with me the same evening. "You see, my son, I had nothing to say about Lai-iu-lut-sa; don't like her myself," said he, with a smile. "Now, had it been Iu-i-tsaih-ti-e-tsa, I should have said, 'Be it well!'" and he waited for me to ask who she was. I kept a wise silence—my old brother kept a sulky one. "She is the finest being in our nation, and *my own niece*," he added, with emphasis.

"I never saw her," said I.

"Is that all?" he exclaimed, eagerly. "Well, she shall bring you a bundle of candle-wood to-morrow evening," he remarked.

"What shall I pay her for it?" I asked.

"Pay her! Nothing, my son; do you wish her to think you a fool, and cover me with shame?"

Next evening I went to see Mr. Graham, the trader, and staid late. When I returned a little bundle of pitch-pine was lying by the doorway, and the old Governor, getting up with an oath, left the house. Again the girl brought wood, at a time unexpected to me, yet I happened to be absent; and the matter, with many vexatious remarks on my strange behavior, was for a time given up.

But the Governor did not despair of getting him a wife, and he finally selected the same Miss Iu-i-tsaih-ti-e-tsa. His Excellency was going to the summer pueblo for a time to look after his crops, and Cushing accompanied him a part of the distance. The young lady was already in the Governor's secret, and very cordially assented to his plans for the match.

"The Zuni customs in courtship are curious. Usually the girl makes the advances. Her parents or friends inform those of the youth, and the latter is encouraged. If suited, he casually drops into the house of the girl, and 'if it be well,' the girl becomes his affianced, or Yi-lu-k'ia-ni-ha (his to be). Thereafter the young couple may be seen frequently together—the girl combing his hair on the sunny terraces, or, in winter, near the hearth, while he sits and sews on articles of apparel for her. When he has 'made his bundle,' or gathered a sufficient number of presents together—invariably including a pair of moccasins made from a whole deer-skin—he takes it to her, and if they are accepted he is adopted as a son by her father, or, in Zuni language, 'as a ward,' *Ta-la-h'i;* and with the beginning of his residence with her he commences his married life. With the woman rests the security of the marriage ties, and it must be said, in her high honor, that she rarely abuses the privilege; that is, never sends her husband 'to the home of his fathers,' unless he richly deserves it. Much is said of the inferior position of women among Indians. With all the advanced tribes, as with the Zunis, the woman not only controls the situation, but her serfdom is customary, self-imposed and willing absolutely. To her belong, also, all the children; and descent, including inheritance, is on her side."

As the Governor and Cushing were leaving the pueblo they met the young lady, Iu-i-tsaih-ti-e-tsa, and the Governor casually hinted that Cushing would be lonely while he was gone. As they parted, a few moments afterward, the Governor talked to him soberly about getting married, and concluded the conversation with this benediction, which Mr. Cushing notes in one of his articles:

"Little brother," said he, and he laid one hand on my shoulder, while with the other he removed his head-band, and pressed both of mine, "*this day we have a father who, from his ancient place, rises hard holding his course; grasping us that we may stumble not in the trails of our lives. If it be well, may his grasp be firm until, happily, our paths join together again and we look one upon the other.* Thus much I make prayer—I go."

With this he turned suddenly, a tear in his eye, and walked hastily along the river-side. And I stood there watching him, until his bent form disappeared, and trying hard to bear the loneliest moment of my exile in Zuni. God bless my Indian brother!

Two days afterward the young lady made the usual advances, and brought a present to him. It was a handsome tray of flaky *he-we*. The Governor's wife disliked the girl very much, and when Cushing returned to the house and found the gift there, he asked her who brought it.

"*You* ask who brought it?" exclaimed the old lady. "Well! Who should it be but that shameless wench who lives over the covered way, whose mother has clog feet, and whose father is so poor that no one knows how they live? No matter if young fools do grow crazy over her; she's nothing, nothing at all, Medicine Flower, nothing but a common creature that is not human enough to know what shame is. She only thinks of what you have and your fine buttons."

Peace was made with the Governor's wife when Cushing

told her he should not accept the advances, and he decided to make short work of this courtship. He went to the house of Iu-i-tsaih-ti-e-tsa, and left word for her to come and eat with him at sunset. "When she came," writes Mr. Cushing, "I was writing. She was accompanied by her aunt. I bade them enter; set coffee, bread, *he-we*, sugar, and other delicacies before them. Then I merely broke a crust, sacrificed some of it to the fire, ate a mouthful, and left them, resuming my writing. The girl dropped her half-eaten bread, threw her head mantle over her face, and started for the door. I called to her and offered her a bag of sugar in payment, I said, for the *he-we*. At first she angrily refused; then bethinking herself that I was an American and possibly knew no better, she took the sugar and hastened away, mortified and almost ready to cry with vexation. Poor girl! I knew I was offering her a great dishonor—as runs the custom of her people—but it was my only way out of a difficulty far more serious than it could have possibly appeared to her people."

Then Mr. Cushing told the Indians of his engagement to a young lady in Washington, and of his intention to marry her and bring her to live with them; and although their preference would have been for him to take a wife from the tribe, their gallantry overcame their prejudice, and they received the pale face, brown-eyed bride with a respectful and cordial welcome.

While the party of Indians were in Washington Mr. Cushing presented them to his fiancee, and they immediately conceived a great fancy for her; but the Governor told him he must not go back to Zuni without taking his bride. She cheerfully consented to accompany him to his pueblo home, and to share his novel experiences.

Mrs. Cushing was the daughter of the late Mr. Magill, who was for many years connected with the venerable banking house of Lewis Johnson & Co., of Washington. Her devotion to her husband runs parallel to his devotion to science, and there are few girls who would leave a beautiful home at Washington for a mud hut in an Indian pueblo, even for men they loved. A man or a woman who does not love luxury fails to reach or realize the privileges and possibilities of existence; but he or she who cannot dispense with luxury and enjoy roughing it is a worthless weakling, unfit for the tasks and the triumphs that the great world offers. Mr. Cushing belongs to that ancient fraternity, the badge of which is always apparent, even under the barbaric costume of the Zuni—the honorable order of gentlemen—and in his rude surroundings and primitive accommodations every sign he gives detects this order to which he belongs, and of which, in Washington or in Zuni, he will always be an ornament.

Mrs. Cushing does not enjoy life in Zuni as her husband does. She does not and cannot share his fascination for the work in which he is engaged. She hates the uncouth women and the naked children, and despises their filthy ways, but she has made her mud hut a pretty little paradise, and has developed the possibilities of comfort even in Zuni.

The clay walls of her rude house are hung with blankets woven by the Zuni and Navajo Indians, and compare in brilliancy of color, texture, and design with the far-famed Gobelin tapestries. The ceilings of undressed trunks of trees are covered with bright figured cretons and Japanese silks. The clay floor is strewn with sheep skins, tanned by the Indians, that are softer to the slippered foot than the rugs of Oriental magnificence, and ornaments selected with refined taste or framed with clever hands after the models of decorative art, are hung here and fastened there, and strewn everywhere. The Cushing residence is a dirty mud hut without, but within a bower of beauty.

She has her sister, Miss Magill, with her, who likes the Zunis better than Mrs. Cushing, and is talking of adopting their peculiar dress and joining their tribe.

"I would do it," said Miss Magill; "it would be so funny and romantic, but I don't like to cut my hair."

The family have a colored man for cook and "maid of all work;" and while their diet is confined to the slender resources of the Indian garden and the provisions of the commissary store at Fort Wingate, all who have visited them can testify to the hospitality, the wholesomeness, and the enjoyment of their table.

CHAPTER III.

A SENATORIAL EPISODE.

THE attempt of certain army officers to deprive the Indians of a portion of their lands has excited newspaper controversy, and attracted much public interest. To understand the situation several important points must be explained.

1. The Zuni Indians have occupied and lived peacefully within the same narrow valley for nobody knows how many centuries. The Spanish invaders found them there when they came 350 years ago, and the Zunis have not left the place since.

2. They are not a migratory tribe, but live in dwellings, cultivate the ground, and have small herds of cattle, sheep, and donkeys. They do not receive and never have received any aid whatever from the government, but are entirely self-supporting, peaceable and happy. It is one of their proudest traditions that they have never killed an "American," as they distinguish the residents of the United States from the Mexicans.

3. Their reservation is almost entirely a barren desert, only a small portion being capable of sustaining herds of cattle, and a limited tract being susceptible of cultivation under a system of irrigation which they have practiced for centuries. They raise corn, wheat, and vegetables in limited quantities, sufficient only for their own sustenance,

and the arable land could not well support more than the number who are now fed from it—about 1,600 people.

4. The entire and absolute value of the Zuni lands depends upon four springs from which they obtain their water supply for themselves, their cattle, and their irrigating ditches. If these springs should be lost, the Zunis must leave the village they have occupied for so many centuries or starve. The government could give them food, but it could not give them water. The two principal springs upon which their water supply depends are known as the Nutrias and the Pescado.

Several years ago, when the railroad approached this locality, the Indian agent at Santa Fe, who exercises a supervisory control over the Zunis, although they receive no government aid, was solicitous about their welfare, and President Hayes directed him to survey and describe the lands occupied and used by the Zunis in order that it might be withdrawn from settlement and exempted from the land grant which Congress had given the Atlantic and Pacific Railroad Company. The agent, Mr. Ben M. Thomas, supposed that he had performed his duty fully, and he, as well as the authorities at Washington and the Zunis themselves, believed that their lands were safe to them forever, and protected against the encroachments of civilization. The military officers at Fort Wingate so understood it, and no one doubts that it was the intention and determination of the government to protect the Zunis in the perpetual possession of their homes, their grazing lands, their farms, and the four springs from which they obtained their water supply. But it appears that there was an unfortunate and lamentable error in the description of the boundary lines. Mr. Thomas explains the manner in which the mistake was made, as follows:

"In 1877 I was directed by the authorities at Washington to furnish a description of the Zuni Reservation. I went over the ground carefully, and through an excess of caution took with me the surveyor who originally laid out the boundary line between New Mexico and Arizona. It was the intention of the government, and of course my own intention, to include in the reservation the lands occupied by the tribe and the springs which supplied them with water. I left the description of the boundaries to the surveyor, not being a practical engineer myself, and he drew an angle from the boundary line of the territory a certain distance, which he said would bring the springs and the Nutrias Valley within the reservation. I am since informed that the angle as designated will fall short and leave them out. Had I been without the assistance of the surveyor I should have described the boundaries by natural landmarks, but supposing that he understood his business I adopted his imaginary lines, and that is the way the mistake was made."

The Indian agent sent his report to Washington, and the following order was issued by President Hayes, defining the Reservation, and withdrawing the land from sale:

EXECUTIVE MANSION, Washington, D. C., March 16, 1877.

It is hereby ordered that the following described tract of country, in the Territory of New Mexico, viz.: Beginning at the 136th mile stone on the western boundary line of the Territory of New Mexico, and running thence north 61 deg. 45 min. east, 31 8-10 miles, to the crest of the mountain a short distance above the Nutrias Spring; thence due south to a point in the hills a short distance southeast of the Ojo Pescado; thence south 61 deg. 45 min. west to the 148th mile stone on the western boundary line of said Territory; thence north with said boundary line to the place of beginning, be and the same is hereby withdrawn from sale and set apart as a reservation for the use and occupation of the Zuni Pueblo Indians. R. B. HAYES.

When the mistake was discovered, two army officers and a citizen located claims of 800 acres each, upon the valley of Las Nutrias, 640 acres under the Desert Land Act, and 160 acres under the Homestead Act. The land officers at Santa Fe accepted the papers, and forwarded them to Washington, with an enquiry as to whether the lands were open to settlement. The following reply was received:

DEPARTMENT OF THE INTERIOR, GENERAL LAND OFFICE,
                Washington, D. C., Dec. 7, 1882.
REGISTER AND RECEIVER, SANTA FE, N. M.

Gentlemen : I am in receipt of your letter of Nov. 23, 1882, asking whether townships 12 n, of rs 16 and 17 w, are within the reservation of the Zuni Indians, as the same are unsurveyed, and you have several applications for desert land entries in said townships.

In reply you are informed that as near as can be ascertained from our records township 12 north, of range 16 west, is outside, while township 12 n, of r 17 w, probably only sections 25, 26, 35, 36, are within the reservation.

When those townships are surveyed the reservation may be found to embrace more of the land than mentioned, and if any desert land entries are found to have been located within the reservation they will be held for cancellation. Very respectfully,
                N. P. MCFARLAND, Commissioner.

When the fact of the entry was discovered by the Indian agent, he submitted the following protest to the department at Washington :

UNITED STATES INDIAN SERVICE, PUEBLO INDIAN AGENCY,
                Santa Fe, N. M. T., April 12.
The Hon. H. PRICE, Commissioner, Washington, D. C.

Sir : I have the honor to acknowledge the receipt of your letter of April 5 marked "L, 3,606, 1883," inclosing letters of the honorable Secretary of the Interior and Commissioner of the General Land Office in regard to entries recently made on the Zuni Reservation. The action taken, as shown by the inclosures, does not reach the real difficulty by any means. The difficulty lies in the manner of regarding the reservation, as shown on the maps, resulting in the contradiction of terms in the description of the boundaries of the reservation. "Beginning at the one hundred and thirty-sixth milestone on the western boundary line of the Territory of New Mexico, and running thence north 61 deg., 45 min. east * * * " does not run that line (the northern) of the reservation "to the crest of the mountain, a short distance above Nutrias Spring;" but leaves out that spring and the Nutrias farms which the Indians have cultivated from time immemorial, and which are necessary to their support. The intention of the reservation was to secure to the Zunis three principal farming districts where they raise the means of subsistence, viz.: Nutrias, Pescado and Ojo Caliente; but in making the original description of the boundaries I was misled by the surveyor who had surveyed the Territorial boundary line, and who was with me at the time I located the reservation. He assured me that the angle "North 61 degrees 45 degrees East" would run the line so as to take in Nutrias; but it seems that it does not. The outrage of taking Nutrias from the Zunis must not be consummated. The thing to do is to follow the apparent intent of the description and run the north line to the crest of the mountain above Nutrias, regardless of the angle given, and then run the eastern line far enough south to take in Pescado Spring, which is still more important to the Indians than Nutria. I trust that you will secure an order to be issued to the Surveyor General of New Mexico to so lay off the reservation. The persons who have taken the preliminary steps to secure the land at Nutrias are mostly army officers, I understand, and one of them assured me to day that if the land was subject to entry by any one they wanted it; but if it belonged to the Indians, and they (the Indians) were to have it, they would not press their claims as against the Indians, provided the money already paid were refunded to them, and their act would not exhaust their right to enter land.

Very respectfully, your obedient servant,

BEN M. THOMAS, United States Indian Agent.

As Surveyor General Atkinson explains the case, the trouble was in the description of the reservation in the executive order of President Hayes; that was very loosely drawn, and its terms are conflicting. Although the intention was clearly to include the springs in the reservation, and they are named in the document, they cannot be included if the angles, distances, and directions stated are preserved. If the natural landmarks as announced are to govern, and the description "by metes and bounds" is to prevail, the farms and springs of the Zunis will be included in the reservation; but if the description "by direction and distance" is accepted, they lie outside the reservation. General Atkinson raises another interesting and important point. He says that in the Gaudaloupe-Hidalgo treaty, under which New Mexico was annexed to the United States, all Indians residing in villages and cultivating the land, were expressly described as citizens, and that they have since been so recognized by the courts. This includes the Zuni tribe, and if the fact is sustained the President had no right to give them a reservation, and they are entitled to no land whatever unless they enter it under the laws. The Indians are not taxed as citizens, however, and never have been regarded or treated as such, either by the National or territorial government.

The Indians were first made aware of the invasion of what they supposed was their own property, by the appearance of a ranchman at the Nutrias spring, who commenced preparations for the establishment of a ranche. They were very much alarmed, and held several excited councils, appealing to Mr. Cushing to assert their rights, but he was powerless to do more than present their side of the case to the authorities. While at Zuni we talked with the old priest, Nai-iu-tchi, concerning the matter, and he showed great grief. He said "my heart is sick with anxiety for my people."

Q. What will you do if the white man does come on your reservation?

A. What do you suppose we can do? It is easy for

the Zuni to grow poor and have trouble. It is easy for the American to grow rich and take our lands away. If there be one thing upon which we depend for our lives, and our cattle, and our corn, it is the four springs. Take those away and you take away the life of the Zuni.

Q. Is that all the water you have?

A. The land of the Zuni is dry and sandy, and those are all the springs we have. We want the water to make food. We do not want to keep others away, but we want the water from the springs in order that we may live.

Q. Have the Zunis always been friendly to the whites?

A. Never, since the time when first our grandfathers grew old enough to have thoughts of their own, has it been known in Zuni that any bad deeds were done by us to the Americans or to us by them. The Navajos, the Apaches and other tribes have wandered off their reservations, but the Zuni always stays at home. They have killed white men, and stolen horses and cattle, and have put on war paint in the face of the Americans, but the Zunis have never killed a white man. They have stayed on their reservations and cultivated the land; unceasingly we be here and we have never borrowed country from others.

Q. You have a letter from President Hayes giving you this reservation?

A. Yes. This is our country, because Washington said it, and he said that the Utes, and the Apaches, and the Navajos should cease to trouble us, and since he said it we go about with our hands hanging at our sides.

The situation was fully explained to the President and

the Secretary of the Interior, and after an examination into its details, the following order was issued:

EXECUTIVE MANSION, May 1.—Whereas, it is found that certain descriptions as to boundaries, given in an executive order issued March 16, 1877, setting apart a reservation in the Territory of New Mexico for the Zuni-Pueblo Indians, are not stated with sufficient definiteness to include within said reservation all the lands specified in, and intended to be covered by, said Executive order, especially the Nutrias Spring and the Ojo Pescado, said executive order is hereby so amended that the description of the tract of land thereby set apart for the purposes herein named shall read as follows:

Beginning at the 136th mile-post, on the west boundary line of the Territory of New Mexico; thence in a direct line to the south-west corner of township 11 north, 18 west; thence east and north following section lines so as to include sections 1, 12, 13, 14, 22, 23, 24, 25, 26, 27, 28, 32, 33, 34, 35, 36 in said township; thence from the northeast corner of said township on range line between ranges 17 and 18 west, and the third connection line north; thence east on said connection line to the northeast section line in range 16, from whence a line due south would include the Zuni settlements in the region of Nutrias and Nutrias Springs and the Pescado Springs; thence south, following section lines to the township lines between townships 9 and 10 north, range 16 west; thence west on said township line to the range line between range 16 and 17 west; thence in a direct line to the 148th mile post on the western boundary line on said Territory; thence north along said boundary line to place of beginning.

CHESTER A. ARTHUR.

The announcement that claims had been located upon the Zuni Reservation was first published in the columns of the Boston *Herald*, the facts being briefly stated in a letter from Santa Fe. This article alleged that Senator John A. Logan was interested in the scheme, one of the parties to file a claim being his son-in-law, W. F. Tucker, recently appointed a paymaster in the United States army. The publication was brought to the attention of Senator Logan by the Washington correspondent of the New York *Times*, who sent the following dispatch to that paper, which was printed in its columns on the 13th of December, 1882:

WASHINGTON, Dec. 12.—A correspondent of a Boston newspaper, writing from Santa Fe, New Mexico, asserts that Senator Logan, of Illinois, has taken steps to secure possession of the Nutria Spring, near the land of the Zuni Indians, and to establish a cattle ranch around it. This correspondent says that the spring has always been regarded as situated on the Zuni reservation, but that recent surveys have shown that by some inadvertency the reservation lines do not include it. It is further said that the Zunis have had possession of the spring for centuries, and that the land around it contains their best wheat-fields, and that to take it away would reduce their agricultural resources one-half, and threaten them with famine. Senator Logan said to-night that he had not taken the land in question. If it was public land, however, he saw no reason why it should not be pre-empted. *He had looked at the land and thought that he would take it if he could get it.*

It was also fully believed and freely asserted at Zuni, Fort Wingate, and other places in the neighborhood, that the Senator was associated with his son-in-law, but he took no public notice of the reports until after the proclamation of the President restoring the lands. Then he addressed an indignant letter to the press, denying that he is interested in the transaction in any way, but defending the right of his son-in-law to the land. Among other things he declared that the disputed valley was not and never had been occupied by the Indians, that they did not need it, nor the springs from which it is watered. They already had more land than enough, and were a dirty, miserable people, unworthy of any regard or attention. He also intimated his intention to appeal from the decision of the President restoring the reservation lines, and further said:

If the recent order that has been issued giving the Zunis 65,000 acres additional stands (which I cannot believe possible after the authorities at Washington investigate and understand this matter) it will cover all the permanent water not now taken in an easterly and westerly direction for a great number of miles, thereby forever preventing the government from making any sales of public lands in that locality. It will also take 32,000 acres of land donated to the Atlantic & Pacific railroad by congress, which has already been platted and offered for sale by the railroad company, as I am informed. How the government will settle with the railroad company in the future it is not for me to determine.

And now I would like to propound one or two questions for any intelligent and fair-minded person to answer.

If a civilized Indian who makes his living by peaceful and agricultural pursuits, being the head of a family, is entitled to over 1,000 acres of land gratuitously, without being required to live on or cultivate it, how much land ought a civilized white man to be entitled to, provided he cultivates it and pays the government price for it?

If a civilized white man can now get only 160 acres of land as a homestead by paying for it, and an Indian can get over 1,000 acres without paying for it, had not the white man better adopt the Cushing plan and become one of the Zuni Indians?

If a white citizen cannot locate a homestead on public land within five miles of the reservation of peaceful and self-sustaining Indians, pray tell how far he must go from their sacred soil in order to make a proper location?

If a Zuni Indian is entitled to 1,000 acres, being the head of a family, without having rendered the government any assistance whatever, and without giving any compensation therefor, how much land should a citizen of the United States be entitled to who has not only been a good citizen but has served his country well in time of war?

Capt. Lawton served gallantly during the war of the rebellion. He located his homestead on the Nutrias Spring; as well also did he locate a desert act claim, adjacent, justly claiming under the law his time of service during the war to count on his homestead location. His locations were not on any Indian land or reservation; he paid the Government price under the law for said land. The question to be answered is, who has the best right to the land in controversy, a soldier by paying for it, or the Indian by asking for it?

The Senator's anxiety lest the railroad company should lose a few acres of the great empire it has received from the Government as a gratuity, is not shared by the officers of that corporation, who are willing to leave the Indians undisturbed in possessson of their ancient heritage; and his apprehensions that the old veterans who paid for homesteads with their loyal blood may not be able to find them on the public domain, is ill-founded as long as millions of square miles of land, infinitely better than that on which the Zunis live, is open to their settlement without disturbing those who now have peaceful and rightful possession. The Indians are entitled to what they need, and no more; and that can be secured them without depriving Captain Lawton or any other gallant soldier, or any other worthy citizen, of a single right or claim he may possess. That the equity of the case is all on the side of the Indians is beyond controversy, and the point to be decided by the Government is, how many centuries must a community occupy and use its lands before a legal title to them can be acquired. If the case were reversed; if a Senator's son-in-law had cultivated his corn, and fed his flocks upon the land in question for three or ten centuries, whether he had a written title to the property or not, an army with banners would be sent to protect him against invasion, and the Senator would laugh at any proposition for his ejectment. No one denies that there was a mistake in the description of the boundary lines; no one doubts that it was the intention of President Hayes to include the disputed valley and springs in the reservation. The question General Logan has raised, is, whether the Indians should suffer and his son-in-law profit by the error of the Indian agent.

General Logan bitterly attacked the personal character and professional reputation of Mr. Cushing, denouncing him as an imposter, and unworthy of belief. It appears that while Mr. Cushing was absent in the east with the Indians, in the summer of 1882, General Logan made a visit to Zuni, and his friends claim that he then and there discovered the young scientist to be a fraud, his articles in the *Century Magazine* to be groundless fiction, and that the ceremonious journey of the Zunis to Boston was a deception and an imposition upon the public. The sacred reeds and gourds and plume sticks which they carried 3,000 miles to fill with water from "the Ocean of the Sunrise" were discovered by the Senator to be vulgar and meaningless vessels, and all their religious demonstrations in the worship of the sacred water to be a flagrant sham.

The object of Mr. Cushing's work among the Zuni Indians was detected to be a morbid desire for notoriety, and the fact that he had been originally employed at the Smithsonian Institution several years ago, to dust the shelves and keep the specimens in order, was offered as evidence of his utter ignorance of the science of ethnology. The work did not stop here. It was a cruel and relentless war against a young man who could not know of the attacks that were being made upon him, and had no means of making a defense of his private character or his professional reputation. So far as can be ascertained, the confidence of the directors of the Smithsonian Institution in Mr. Cushing and their faith in the integrity of his character and his work was not impaired. The petty spite and the selfish motive that inspired the war upon him was too apparent to be influential, and for a long time Mr. Cushing was totally ignorant that his reputation had been assailed and his fidelity questioned.

The evidence advanced to show that he is an imposter and a writer of falsehoods in the name of science was based upon the investigation made by General Logan's party at Zuni during a two hours' visit while Mr. Cushing was absent. The General's friends relate with sober faces the fact that he asked an old man if it was not true that

Cushing was a fraud, and the Indian nodded his head in assent. The distinguished Senator then asked him if Cushing was not a worthless and a wicked man, and if all the stories he had written about Zuni in the magazine were not lies, and again the Indian nodded acquiescence, as if a savage who never knew the meaning of a written word, was familiar with *The Century* and the Smithsonian reports. This convincing conversation was carried on with no interpreter but a lady who had visited Zuni but twice before and understood little if any of the language, which it has required Cushing three years of constant study to master.

The Senator has recently, over his own signature, denounced Mr. Cushing in the most violent language, with no other reason than that the latter was supposed to have assisted in some way to thwart the schemes of the Senator's son-in-law. Mr. Willard L. Metcalf, a well-known artist of Boston, who was sent to Zuni by the publishers of *The Century* magazine to make the illustrations for Mr. Cushing's articles, and having spent many months there, knows more of the tribe, its condition, its necessities, its customs and its history, than any one except Mr. Cushing, replied to Senator Logan's assault upon his associate by saying: "A man who would make such a narrow and bigoted statement as that (referring to the Senator's published letter) I would not attempt to answer. It carries its own condemnation with it. Any man who knows Cushing, or any man outside of those interested in this scheme to get the springs and lands away from the Zunis, would laugh at it. Cushing is doing a noble work for science. He has nearly ruined his health, in his self-sacrificing labor, but it goes for naught with him in case he is allowed to continue to the end, which he now thinks is approaching. He believes that his work will prove very valuable to ethnological science, and that he will establish conclusively that the Zunis are the true descendants of the Aztecs. Cushing had no thought of arousing the anger of Logan, and was only desirous to be permitted to remain undisturbed among the Zunis until able to complete his studies of them and their traditions. He knows, however, as does every one else acquainted with the country, that the taking away of the springs from the Zunis will necessitate their removal, as without the springs the country would be almost entirely barren and unproductive."

In reply to Senator Logan's assertion that the Indians have plenty of land and water without the disputed tract, Mr. Metcalf says: "General Logan must have been sadly misinformed in some particulars and grossly deceived in others. In regard to his own observations I can only say that he visited the Nutrias Valley at the wrong season of the year to see the Indians. They reside most of the time in Zuni. When the time comes for planting Zuni is almost deserted. The people move out bag and baggage into the Nutrias and the other valleys, stay a month or six weeks until the crops are in and started, and then go back to the pueblo. They go out again to harvest. Their chief crop is corn, but they also raise some wheat, onions, and other vegetables. The latter are generally cultivated in small gardens. The water from the Nutrias and Pescado Springs unite and form the Zuni River, and the loss of either of these sources of supply would almost imperil the existence of the river itself. Before the issuance of the President's proclamation the land around Nutrias Spring was known as 'Logan's land,' and its advantages as the headquarters of a large cattle ranche was frequently discussed at Fort Wingate. In these conversations it was often canvassed how many cattle the spring would supply, and it was an understood thing that the spring was to be dammed so as to make a reservoir for the cattle business. It would be necessary to do this to make the spring available for stock. In addition to the Nutrias and Pescado, there is a small spring nine or ten miles from Zuni, where one can scarcely water a horse. Then there is the Ojo Caliente, twenty-five miles south. These and a small drinking spring in the pueblo form the entire water supply for that country. From this you can see how terrified the Zuni must have been when they learned that one of their largest springs, furnishing fully one-third of their entire supply, was to be taken away by Logan."

Mr. Cushing carefully avoids taking any part in the discussion with General Logan, and has maintained a dignified silence under the latter's attacks upon him, but has succeeded in quieting the Indians with assurances that the President, or "the Great Father Washington," as they call him, would protect them in their rights. It is believed that the Spanish authorities two or three centuries ago gave the Zunis, and other Pueblo tribes, written titles to their land, and that the record still exists somewhere. In his report of a visit to Zuni in 1853, while making a survey of New Mexico for railway purposes, Lieut. Ives, of the army, speaks of seeing some curious old Spanish manuscripts in the home of the Cacique, which were written upon parchment and bore an ancient date. As nearly as could be ascertained they had been handed down from generation to generation of priests, until they were considered very precious. Lieutenant Ives was not permitted to handle or copy them, as the Cacique feared such sacrilege might bring evil upon the people. Mr. Cushing is aware of the existence of some such documents in the tribe to-day, but as yet has not been able to secure them. They are supposed to be a grant from the Spanish Government to the Indians of the land they now occupy, and may be useful in the event that the attempt to rob them of the Nutrias Valley should be persisted in.

Mr. W. H. H. Davis, who was the first United States District Attorney for New Mexico, from 1849 to 1854, once wrote a very valuable and interesting work upon the Pueblo Indians of the Territory, which is regarded as high authority, and is freely quoted by Schoolcraft, Bancroft and other historians. With reference to this subject, Mr. Davis says:

"Soon after the conquest by Cortez, the government became sensible of the policy of conciliating a people so numerous and powerful as the aborigines of the country, and hence grants of land were made to the respective Pueblos for purposes of agriculture.

"The first decree upon this subject is that of Charles V., given in 1523, only three years after the conquest, which authorizes and directs the viceroys and governors to grant to each village as much land as might be necessary for agricultural and building purposes.

"The next decree is that of 1533, which makes the mountains, pastures and waters common to both Spaniards and Indians.

"On the 21st of March, 1551, the Emperor Charles promulgated a third ordinance touching the Pueblo Indians, but which concerned their spiritual more than their temporal welfare.

"The decree of Felipe II., of June, 1587, confirmed to each of the different Pueblos a grant of eleven hundred square varas of land, to be measured from the last house in the village toward the four points of the compass. The quantity was afterward increased to a league square."

When the news of the proclamation of President Arthur was received at Zuni, the entire village shouted for joy, and old Nai-iu-tchi, the priest, sent for Cushing to write for him a letter to "the Washington." Mr. Cushing took his pencil, and wrote at the priest's dictation, as follows:

"I speak to my father as though he were a Zuni and a visitor within my door:

"Father, you have thrown the light of your favor upon a nation small and poor, yet, with the gratitude of a grander and wealthier nation, I speak the thanks of my children to you this day. My brothers and I had the sublime fortune to grasp your warm hand and breathe upon it and from it, and to listen to your words and those of your chiefs in the great pueblo of Washington; and although to-day we do not hear those words or grasp that warm hand, yet, as if we heard them, they ring in our ears and rest in our hearts.

"Father, ever since I visited you in your house of gold and white stone you have been with me and I have been with you as if we were in one house. Though far asunder, I have dwelt with you since that day. It has been said, and I have heard it, that our lands and waters would be taken from us, and, I said to myself, when our pueblo eats up the substance of another, whither will the inhabitants of the other go? Will they, who are men, become dogs, and sit at the doorways of the other, owned and yet disowned, fed and yet hungry? I have heard the one pueblo is the nation of the Americans, the other is the nation of the Zunis. No, the father would not suffer his children to become as dogs at the doors of strangers. And we have a father.

"Father, through your will we are this day happy, when but for your will we had been heavy with thoughts. Thank you, our father.

"May the sun of all summers that number your years find you as happy as were your Zuni children when they listened to the words of you and your chiefs—words which sounded to their ears and to their hearts as beautiful as to the eyes look a vale of flowers."

When men talk of civilization they mean the measure of aggregated human experience,—liberty, morality, industry, humanity and justice; generosity to the weak, resistance to oppression, and self confidence toward the strong. If that be civilization the Zunis have it to a higher degree than some of our law-givers.

CHAPTER IV.

SOME STRANGE COINCIDENCES AND CURIOUS CUSTOMS.

TO decide the age of Zuni would be to terminate a discussion that has been going on for three hundred and fifty years. It puzzled the Spaniards of the time of Cortez, as it puzzles the ethnologists of the Smithsonian Institute to-day. There are theories enough, almost as many as the number of those who have studied the question, and sufficient evidence to convince the learned pundits that its people are the oldest upon the American continent, now in the fading twilight of their existence, almost as old and weary as the land upon which they live; but who they are, whence they came, and how they gained their knowledge of the mechanic and agricultural arts, is a problem no mortal mind can solve. It is known that the pueblo at present occupied by them was erected after the Spanish invasion of 1540, when old Zuni was destroyed, and its inhabitants driven to the mountains to escape punishment for no crime except that of defending their own households; but the original town bore the rust and wrinkles of centuries when Cabaza de Vaca first saw it in 1530, and the report of Coronado, the invader, who visited the place at the head of his army ten years after, regards its antiquity with wonder and awe. Later investigations have discovered that even old Zuni stood upon a heap of ruined walls, which must have been centuries old when the town, whose age no one can number, was begun.

When I asked the old priest Nai-iu-tchi how long his people had been at Zuni, he replied: "So long that could any one tell it, the reply would be, How long was that?" and then he went on to say, that they had been there "since the time when our fathers were born from the womb of the earth. When they came here they brought with them the scalp of a great priest, which was as full of hair as my own head. Eight hundred years after they came, the world was filled with water, and they went into the mountains for safety. They carried the scalp with them, and each year they sacrificed a hair. More generations ago than I could count on all my fingers the last hair was sacrificed. Then my people thought the world would turn over, but it didn't turn over. In comparison to that time it was only a few days ago that the ancient Washington came and asked us to show him the roads to the springs of the Navajos. (This is a reference to Lieutenant Ives' exploration in 1853.) We passed over the plains and the hills covered with pines to a canon filled with sage brush and yellow tops and flags. It was a little country like a bowl, and in the center was a spring, and we called it the country of flags—I mean cat tails. There the Americans sat down and they held a council and built a town."

There are other old pueblos whose origin cannot be fixed, but around Zuni the most interest clusters. The traditions in the several villages generally differ; at least three, and, perhaps, four languages are spoken among them; their modes of worship and mythology bear but little resemblance, but upon some points, and the more essential ones, they show fraternal relations, and undoubtedly are the children of the same sire. The traditions in all the tribes are that they came from a far country, and that when they die they will return whence their fathers came; they have prophets who receive revelations; they have fast days on which they abstain from food and drink. They possessed the knowledge of irrigation and were using it when their existence was discovered; and the ruins which lie all over an area of many thousand square miles show not only that their population was at one time very large, but that nations extinct for centuries practiced irrigation in agriculture also. They grew tobacco long before Captain John Smith discovered it in Virginia, and taught the Spaniards how to make cigarettes, using the corn husk for wrappers; they cultivated wheat and maize when the Spaniards found them, ground it into flour, and baked their dough as it was done in the time of Abraham; they have cotton, the same kind that is produced in Egypt, and they spin and weave it on the same sort of looms that are seen in the pictured Bibles. Their plows and their ox-carts are described by Josephus, and they thresh their grain as the good old prophets used to do. Their pottery is of the same form and bears the same decorations as the antique Egyptian wares, and in some of the old sacred caves there are relics to show that their fathers possessed at least a meager knowledge of the mechanic arts. They had cattle and sheep when the Spaniards came here, and the trustful burro which has been their beast of burden for centuries, is the same patient, enduring donkey that carries the tourist through the streets of Jerusalem to-day.

Zuni is a fragment of Syria, darkly bronzed. The customs of the people are more like those of the Syrians than those of the ordinary North American Indian; their language, their salutations, their social deferences, their etiquette is all oriental, and their speeches read like the poetry of Persia. Some of their fables are almost identical with those of Æsop, and their religious ceremonials are strikingly similar to those of the Egyptians.

In the extreme southeastern corner of Utah are some wonderful ruins which show that they were inhabited by an enlightened race of people, centuries ago, and the traditions of the Zunis indicate a probability that their forefathers once resided in that direction. The ruins lie in the fertile valley of the Animas, and show the remains of houses, corrals, fortifications, irrigation ditches, and pottery ware. The houses were built of sand stone, cemented with mud, very much in the same style of the pueblos of to-day. The finest of the ruins, as described by Professor Hayden, are about thirty-five miles below Animas City, where the valley at one time was literally covered with buildings of every size, the two largest being 300 by 6,000 feet. The outer walls are sand stone laid in adobe, four feet thick, while the interior division walls are built in the same manner, being from six inches to three feet thick. No signs of doors appear, and the dwellings must have been entered from the top with ladders, as is the custon nowadays. That the builders had axes of some kind is shown by the cedar poles that were cut and hewn before being placed in the buildings. The inside walls and ceilings were once white washed and covered with decorations, drawings and inscriptions. In one of the rooms the impression of a human hand, dipped in white wash and then placed upon the brown wall, is as plain as if only made yesterday. In some of the rooms have been found human bones, bones of animals, corn cobs, straw, cigarettes, leather, tanned and raw, and all colors and variety of pottery. Portions of the village were once destroyed by fire, the timbers having burned out and the roofs caved in. Around the village are old irrigating ditches. The Indian traditions point to a residence in these ruins about 600 years ago, and the probability is that the inhabitants were overcome, driven out or slaughtered by the savage Ute Indians, who also have traditions of wars for the extermination of their enemies.

Senor Altamirano, of Mexico, said to be the best Aztec scholar living, disputes the theory that the Aztecs radiated from the Garden of Eden at the time of the scattering of the nations, and argues that they were a race as old as the Asiatics themselves, and the probability is that the other continent was peopled from this. The ruins in Colorado, Utah, Arizona and New Mexico can be traced in a continuous chain along the inhabitable valleys to Mexico, where they culminate in massive and imposing structures, as if that place had been the end of the exodus. In the San Luis valley, of Northern New Mexico, where the Rio Grande river is snow born in the mountains of the Sangre del Christo range, are some wonderful cave dwellings—a colony, at an altitude of 8,000 feet above the sea, and two and a half miles from the nearest water. Appearances indicate that these dwellings were inhabited when the San Luis valley was an immense lake, and the question is asked, while that great valley was filled with water, where was the rest of America? The valley is 7,000 feet above the ocean, and when it was submerged most of the continent must have been the bottom of a sea. It is easy to follow these cave dwellers, according to the theory of Senor Altamirano, as they passed southward, apparently following the receding waters, a generation at a time, at intervals of centuries, and stopping for ages in the places where their ruins now lie, along the rivers of the La Plata, Mancos, San Juan, Gila and the Colorado, reaching Mexico at the end of their march and erecting the Aztec Empire.

Baron von Humboldt fixed New Mexico and Colorado as the region inhabited by the Aztecs in the tenth century, and believed that the Pueblo Indians are from them descended. Other scientists theorize that they must be remnants of Toltec colonies; but to go back of the Aztecs and Toltecs, where did they come from, and how did they learn what they know? It is the opinion of other learned men that their fathers crossed the Behring Straits from Asia, and brought with them the customs and the cattle, the plowshares and the sheep, the poetic idioms and the burros of the Orient.

Another curious theory has been advanced, and has found its way into so orthodox a work as Schoolcraft's History of the Indians; and it is that the Zunis sprang from a party of Welsh navigators who went off with Prince Madoc in the twelfth century, and were never heard from again. Curiously enough, some of the words of the Zuni language are similar in meaning and in sound to those of the Welsh, but this is not the case in any of the other pueblos, and is the only straw to which these ingenious theorists cling. Perhaps there is one other, however, in the presence at Zuni of several albinos, with perfectly white hair, blue eyes, and a dead white complexion which exposure to the sun does not darken. Dr. Tenbroek, of the United States army, who visited Zuni in 1851, saw traces of Welsh features in the physiognomy of these albinos, and caught in their conversation the tongue-twisting consonants of the language of Wales. At that time Dr. Tenbroek says that Zuni had 4,000 inhabitants —to-day it has only 1,600. Lieutenant Ives, of the army, who visited Zuni in 1853, says that the presence of albinos was explained by the Mexican guide by a tradition, which he admits is too vague for credence, that several centuries ago a company of Welsh miners coming northward from Mexico were killed by the Zunis and their wives and children retained as members of the tribe. This, the Lieutenant says, is the only explanation he could gather of the presence of the Welsh accent in the vocabulary, and the Welsh features in the faces of the albinos of the tribe; but there are albinos in other pueblos as well as Zuni. In describing his visit to Moquis, Lieutenant Ives says: "A woman with a fair white complexion has been in camp this morning. It seems incredible that she should be of Indian parentage, but such cases are by no means rare in the pueblos of New Mexico."

It seems scarcely reasonable to found a theory of Zuni origin upon these two circumstances, and the fact that a party of Welshmen sailed away and never came back again. The Zunis have no tradition referring either to the Welsh navigators or to taking the wives and children of murdered Welsh miners into their tribe. I saw one albino at Zuni, a monstrous fellow, with a pallid face that was covered with freckles. He seemed to avoid observation, but such as he are treated well by the Indians. The governor has a nephew who is an albino—the son of tawny parents. He is the pet of the family and receives much deference, as cripples do in the households of civilization. There seems to be the same sort of superstition about these lonesome oddities that there is in the savage tribes regarding persons who are insane.

The Zunis have an unwritten epic, like the Iliad of Homer, which is intrusted to the memory of a priest, who has nothing to do but to remember its lines and recite them upon occasions when such a ceremony is in order. He is a sort of bard or historian for the tribe, and is supported at public expense. In order that by no accident or fatality the legend should be lost, this priest has four assistants, who are selected from the tribe and taught the lines by the old man, so that they may be competent to assist him in the recitals and succeed him when his days are over. Chapters from this bible are recited upon different public occasions, at the feasts and the fasts, but it is seldom repeated entire.

The work begins with the mythical origin of the people, and then enters into what may be considered accurate tradition and genuine history. It is in perfect rhyme and rythm and abounds in the same poetic orientalism that adorns all the utterances of the Zunis. The recitals regarding the invasion of Coronado compare very accurately with the conqueror's own reports, and the description of the places where their forefathers lived centuries previous to the conquest, corresponds with the location of famous ruins, which the Indians for several generations back, at least, could not possibly have visited. Every place to which their bible refers as the deserted dwellings of the people can be identified with unerring accuracy by those familiar with the ruins of Arizona.

The old, blind priest, who, until death released him, was the keeper of the traditions, related the genesis of the tribe to Mr. Cushing in the following beautiful legend:

In the days of the new, after the time when all mankind had come forth from one to the other of the "four great cavern wombs of earth" (a-wi-ten-te-huthl-na-kwin), and had come out into the light of our father, the sun, they journeyed, under the guidance of A-hai-iu-ta and Ma-tsai-le-ma, twin children of the sun, immortal youths, toward the father of all men and things, eastward.

In those times a day meant four years, and a night the same; so that, in the speech of the ancients, "Between one sunrise and another," meant eight years.

After many days and nights the people settled near the Mountain of the Medicine Flower, and a great cacique sent forward his two children, a young man and a young girl—the passing beautiful of all children—to explore for a better country. When they had journeyed as far as the region where now flow the red waters (Colorado Chiquito) they paused to rest from their journey. Ah! they sinned and were changed to a demon god and goddess.

The world was damp. Plant corn on the mountain tops, and it grew. Dig a hole into the sands at will, and water filled it.

The woman in her anger drew her foot through the sands, that she might—from shame—separate herself from her people; and the waters, collecting, flowed off until they were a deep channel; yet they settled most about the place where she stood, and it became a lake which is there to this day. And the mark in the sands is the valley where now flow the red waters.

No tidings came from the young messengers, and after many days the nation again journeyed eastward, carrying upon their backs not only their things precious but also their little children. When they reached the waters they were dismayed; but some ventured in to cross over. Fear filled the hearts of many mothers, for their children grew cold and strange, like others than human creatures, and they dropped them into the waters, changed indeed; and they floated away crying and moaning, as ever now they cry and moan when the night comes on and the hunter camps near their shores. But those who loved their children and were strong of heart passed safely over the flood and found them the same as before.

Thus it came to be that only part of our nation ever arrived at the "middle of the world." But it is well, as all things are; for others were left to remember us and to make a home, not of strangers, but of "our others," for those who should die and to intercede with the "Holders of the Waters of the World" that all mankind and unfinished creatures, even flying and creeping beings, might have food to eat and water to drink when the world should harden and the land should dry up. And in that lake is a descending ladder, down which even the smallest may enter fearlessly who has passed its borders in death; where it is delightful, and filled with songs and dances; where all men are brothers, and whence they wander whither they will, to minister to and guide those whom they have left behind them; that is the lake where live "our others," and whither go our dead. At night he who wanders on the hills of the Ka-ko'k-shi may sometimes see the light shining forth and hear strange voices of music coming up from the depths of those waters.

The Moquis, who live in Arizona, seventy miles northwest of Zuni, have a legend that the earth was once a small island, inhabited by one man, whose father was the sun, and whose mother was the moon; that the gods sent a wife to him to cheer his loneliness, and that the earth grew as their family multiplied. The children became dissatisfied and restless after years, began to wander, and built up towns. Visits between them became infrequent, and finally ceased, until in generations their common ancestry was forgotten. Centuries ago a war broke out between the Pueblo, or permanent Indians, and the wandering tribes, and the former were driven to the rocks and caves, where they built nests like wrens and swallows, erecting fortifications and watch-towers, dug reservoirs in the rocks to catch the rain-fall, and held their enemies at bay. The besiegers were beaten back, but the hollows in the rocks were filled with blood, and it poured in torrents through the canons. It was such a victory that they dare not try again, and when the fight was over they wandered to the southward, and in the deserts of Arizona, on isolated, impregnable bluffs, they built new towns, and their descendants, the Moquis, live in them to this day.

The Navajos, a mighty tribe which inhabits the country between the Zuni and Moquis, and around them both, have their own novel theory of the origin of man. It goes that in the beginning all men lived in the center of the earth. One day a Navajo accidentally touched the top of the cave and heard a hollow sound, which awakened their curiosity and tempted them to dig through the ground. After digging some distance they found they were nearing the top, and they sent a raccoon up as a pioneer. He failed to make any progress, and, coming down discouraged, an earth worm was put in his place. He bored a hole through the earth into the air, and sat down to rest awhile, when he discovered four great swans at the four cardinal points, each bearing an arrow under its wing. The swan from the north first rushed upon him, and, having thrust his arrow through the body of the worm, retired. This was repeated by the other three. The worm being frightened, went back into his hole with the arrows still through his body. This made the hole large enough for the raccoon to climb up, and after him followed the men. At that time there was no heaven, neither was there sun, moon, or stars. It was determined that these were essential to the comfort and convenience of the Navajos, so a council of old and wise men was called to manufacture them. When the sun was finished it was placed in position on the top of a rock, and the priests puffed smoke in its face. It commenced to rise, and they kept blowing until it reached its present position.

Nearly every water course, every spring, and every empty canon where a stream has sometime been, in the whole territory, from the grand continental divide to the Colorado river, have about them evidences that an enormous population once inhabited this dreary waste. Often the ruined walls of cities are found remote from water, and the topography of the country gives additional testimony that the streams which fed them centuries ago have either changed their course or ceased to exist. Around these ruins are scattered innumerable fragments of broken pottery, and that they were once the dwellings of a peaceful and agricultural people is shown by the irrigating ditches, or acequias, which lead from the valleys to the dry beds of gravel, where the water has once been.

A few miles east of Zuni is a quadrangular mass of white sand stone, known as Inscription Rock, which has attracted much attention. It is nearly a mile in length, and more than 200 feet in height. Upon its weather-beaten surface are numerous inscriptions in Spanish, cut by persons who have passed that way, some of them deeply and beautifully engraved, and dated as far back as 1606. Upon the top of the rocks are the ruins of two pueblos the size and shape of which can be distinctly traced, and many pieces of painted pottery are lying about. The inscriptions often contain short histories of the object of the visit of those by whom they were engraved; either explorers of the country, Spanish soldiers on the march to the conquest, or early Franciscan friars penetrating the wilderness to convert the native heathen to the living God. What a field for sober reflection and poetic romance this rock presents to the mind with its inscriptions and its ruined villages! It is a mute but eloquent historian of an unknown past.

In 1853 Lieutenant Whipple and Lieutenant Ives, of the corps of Topographical Engineers, made an exploration of the thirty-fifth parallel under an act of Congress directing a survey for the purpose of ascertaining the most practicable route across the continent for a railroad. The line these gentlemen followed is very nearly that adopted by the Atlantic and Pacific company for their road already in operation west of Albuquerque, and its proposed eastern extension to St. Louis. These officers left Fort Smith, Ark., crossed the Indian Territory and New Mexico, and in November, 1853, reached Zuni, where they spent some days. The tribe had recently been ravaged by small-pox and half the population carried off, so that the occasion was not a favorable one to see the town. This accounts for the reduction of the population, which Dr. Tenbroek gives as 4,000 in 1851, to the 1,600 that exist there to-day. When Coronado made his famous march the Zunis must have numbered many thousands of people, although no estimate of their population is given by him. There were seven cities of Zuni then, only two of which are to-day inhabited; five were destroyed or have yielded to the tooth of time. Another has since been built, and that is the Zuni of to-day. Oppression and pestilence, wars with the Apaches and Navajos and a disregard of sanitary laws, have diminished their number to a mere handful, compared to the tribe they once were, and the entire nation will soon be extinct. They are nothing now but a few peaceful people, invested with a most remarkable sense of the poetic, and having the custody of volumes of beautiful ideas and traditions.

The coat of arms of the Zuni Nation is the Sacred

Water Spider (Shi-wi-nas), and this symbol, engraven upon the rocks and walls of ruined towns ages ago, is evidence in addition to that already noted, of the extent and multitude of their kindred and ancestry, whose decayed and forsaken houses furnish one of the most absorbing studies for the scientist of this generation. Curiously enough, when the archæologists who are examining these heaps of stone send to the Smithsonian Institute the results of their researches, and the theories which their investigations enable them to frame, they are found to correspond approximately, if not always accurately, with the traditions Mr. Cushing pumps out of the reticent priests who jealously treasure their proud history.

The Zuni of to-day is the largest of all the pueblos of New Mexico and Arizona, and with the exception of the Moquis and the Kuhnis tribe of Arizona, is the least known and most isolated. The latter tribe, sometimes called the Java Supais, occupy a small and almost inaccessible village in one of the canons of the Colorado, and is so far unknown that its name does not even appear in the official list of Indian nations. The Pueblos of the Rio Grande reverence Zuni, as the oldest member of their family, the least tainted with the hateful and hated Mexican, and the unadulterated remnant of the Aztec source from which their religion and their peculiar institutions sprang.

The four Zuni villages are Zuni, Las Nutrias, Pescado and Ojo Caliente, the three latter being known as the farming Pueblos, being situated near springs of the same names, and in valleys whose soil is fertile, and can be reached by irrigating ditches. They may be called the country villas, or summer resorts of the tribe, for during the winter the houses are nearly all sealed up, and the entire population, except a few families who are left on guard, retire to Zuni until the planting season shall come again. One of the most curious customs they have is this sealing up of their houses, which are usually entered from the roof, through a sort of scuttle hole, by going up one ladder from the ground and down another to the floor. They have no bolts or locks or bars, but when a citizen retires to his country residence for the summer, or leaves the latter for city life in the fall, he spreads a bundle of straw upon the entrance to his dwelling, and smears it over with a thick coating of mud, upon which, at the proper place, some mark or seal is impressed that is known only to the owner.

Las Nutrias is a collection of about sixty houses, piled up in terraces, as all the Pueblos are, and is surrounded with queer looking corralls, where the beasts are kept, that resemble a girdle of thorns. It is sixteen miles from Zuni and is the principal farming Pueblo. Around it is a fine pasture and a fertile soil. The cultivated plats are fenced off to protect the gardens from the cattle and sheep, and upon them are raised wheat, corn, onions, garlic and other toothsome vegetables. The crop of peppers is always very large, and never fails, for they compose the principal ingredient of the hideous mixtures which form the Zuni diets. A very accurate idea of the taste of burning brimstone can be obtained by swallowing a mouthful of one of the most delicate dishes of their menu, composed of mutton boiled in peppers and garlic. It was such stuff as this that ruined Mr. Cushing's stomach, which suffered martyrdom until he became so firmly entrenched in the tribe as to safely insist upon cooking his own food and getting his rations from the Army Commissary at Fort Wingate.

Another dainty dish of the Zuni cuisine is roasted locusts. It usually strikes one with repugnance, but there ought to be no more objection to eating locusts than shrimps. To catch them, the holes where the locust larvæ lie are watched in the early morning. Just as the first rays of the sun strike the earth, they all appear simultaneously, as if at a signal call. The ground is suddenly covered with them, and they are captured by thousands, and taken home in baskets and bowls. They are put to soak in cold water, and left to stand over night. This fattens them, and in the morning they are roasted in a dish over the fire, the mass being continually stirred until it becomes a uniform brown.

Parched corn is a staple article of diet. The cuticle is removed by boiling it in lye, and it is then parched upon hot stones, being quite palatable to the taste. The corn is also parched a little before it is ground into meal, and is then baked in the dome-shaped ovens of stone and mud that stand around the villages, and are often seen upon the housetops. The same method of grinding flour is in vogue in all the pueblos, and has its counterpart in the customs of the early Egyptians, as almost every characteristic of the Indians is linked by some resemblance to the early races of scriptural history. A row of girls, three, four, or five, are generally seen grinding together, —the Bible says that "two women were grinding at the mill." They all kneel beside a series of small bins, each of which has a stone bottom worn as smooth as glass by friction, either concave in shape, or lying at an angle of 40 degrees. Each girl has a bar of stone in her hands, and crushes the corn between that and the bottom of the bin by rubbing it up and down as clothes are rubbed upon a washboard. The corn or wheat is put into the first bin and ground a while, when it is put into the second, and so on until it becomes as soft and fine as that produced by the modern processes of civilization. The girls have well developed muscles, and crush the grain with an energy that is commendable. They make a pretty picture as they bend over their work, with their glossy black hair tossing to the rythm of their motion and their roguish eyes looking out from under it in a most coquettish way. Very often they carry a baby strapped upon the back, which sleeps as soundly and solemnly through the process as if it were cuddled in a cradle.

There are two kinds of bread made at Zuni; the "he-we," and "he-per-lo-ki." Both are notably peculiar. The latter looks, and is said by the few who have tried it, to taste like Boston brown bread, but the manner in which it is made does not recommend it to civilized palates, the coarse, unbolted corn meal being chewed by the cook before it is baked. The object of this, singularly enough, is to sweeten it, the acid of the saliva, when united with the starch of the corn, forming a sort of glucose that is said to contain a high degree of saccharine. Some of the tribe, including the Governor's family, follow this process no longer; Mr. Cushing, during the time he boarded with them, having demonstrated the advantage of sugar over the natural process. After being thoroughly chewed it is moistened with water, kneaded in an earthen bowl, and baked between corn husks. It is heavy as lead, and looks indigestible, but those who have had the courage to eat it declare that it is agreeable to the taste, and causes no distress to the stomach. The other class of bread, "he-we," is quite as curious in its appearance and manner of manufacture, and resembles the *marros* of the Hebrews. Fine meal is mixed with water until it forms a thin paste, when it is smeared over a very hot stone slab with a quick motion of the hand. It is baked almost instantly, the stone being so hot and the dough so thin. As soon as done, the sheets are laid one above the other until they form a considerable pile. They are in various tints, blue, pink, green, and yellow, according to the color of the corn, which is sorted when shelled, with a view to securing this effect. This bread is eaten dry and has a pleasant, wafery taste. It is also eaten by dipping rolls of it into mutton broth. In his visit to Moquis in 1857 Lieut. Ives describes this bread. He says: "Our host courteously asked us to be seated upon some skins spread along the floor against the wall, and presently his wife brought in a vase of water and a tray filled with a singular substance that looked more like sheets of thin blue wrapping paper rolled into bundles than anything else. I afterward learned that it was made from corn meal, ground very fine, made into a gruel and poured over a heated stone to be baked. When dry it has a highly polished surface like paper. The sheets are folded and rolled together, and form the staple article of food with the Zuni Indians. As the dish was intended for our entertainment and looked clean, we all partook of it. It had a delicate fresh bread flavor, and was not at all unpalatable, particularly when eaten with salt."

The pueblo of Las Nutrias, with its spring and gardens, lies in the disputed portion of the Zuni Reservation. The next largest farming pueblo is Pescado, an older town than Zuni, which at one time was of considerable population and importance, but is now only a temporary residence during the farming season for a portion of the tribe who have their gardens there. The name Pescado means fish, and the village is so called from the fact that in the spring, which gushes out of a great lava rock near by, are a few peculiar representatives of the finny tribe. Though eating many strange things, the Zunis will not touch fish; not from a lack of appetite, but from religious scruples, as every thing that lives in the water, which they worship, is as sacred as a crucifix. Around Pescado are a few small farms or gardens, one of which belongs to Mr. Cushing's "brother," the Governor. This village and spring is also in the disputed territory.

The third village is Ojo Caliente, so named from a spring of warm water, which also finds its source in the lava rock, and is undoubtedly heated by the same subterranean fires that warm the waters of similar fountains which have been discovered in other portions of the territory.

At Zuni village, outside of the corrals in which the animals are kept, are the queer little gardens which supply fresh vegetables and herbs during the summer, and are cultivated by the women. They are separated by curious looking fences, built of stakes driven into the ground, closely together, and sometimes by walls of stone or adobe. The little inclosures are cut up into rectangular beds, and before the seeds sprout, look like brown waffles. They are irrigated entirely by hand, it being the duty of the boys and girls of the family each morning to bring a jar of water from the spring and empty it in the little ditch that surrounds each bed.

The ground is ploughed with just such an arrangement as the Egyptians used, pictures of which can be seen in the illustrated Bibles, and Rollin's Ancient History. The valleys are easily tilled, and need only moisture to produce enormous crops. The corn is planted by punching holes in the ground with a stick, and the wheat is sown by the same method that civilized farmers use. All the farming labor is done by men, with the exception of tending the gardens at Zuni, as the pueblo tribes do not consider manual labor within the sphere of woman. In this they differ from all the other Indians in America.

The Zunis are indolent and take life easy, like the Mexicans, and all the other residents of their climate; but they are not lazy, and are wonderfully systematic and methodical in their labors. They are constitutionally a happy and contented people, require but little here below, and are able to gain it without much toil. A few cattle and sheep, an acre or two of land is all they need to sustain life; and it is well that this is so, for ninety-nine per cent. of the area they occupy is a barren desert, incapable of sustaining anything but lizards and horned toads, which produce in profusion. The men, as well as the women, are great gossips, and sit around in the shady places dozing and dreaming, or talking of the glories of the past.

The women spin, weave, and knit, make pottery, and bake bread. One of the most interesting sights to be seen at Zuni is the weaving of their woolen fabrics, blankets, and clothing, on their curious hand looms, which are two poles, one suspended from the ceiling and the other attached to the floor. They produce beautiful and accurate designs without patterns, and with no measurement but the eye. Their brilliant and imperishable colors are secured by the use of roots, herbs, and the offal of animals. The Navajos produce the finest blankets in the world, which the looms of civilization have never been able to equal. The Zunis have not the art to so great perfection as the Navajos, but their blankets are beautiful, and are so tightly woven as to hold water. Each family makes its own pottery, as well as clothing; and some of the women are adepts in the moulding and decoration of jars, pitchers, and bowls. The work is finely glazed, and although fragile, is easily replaced when broken.

The Zuni houses have large rooms, and are scrupulously clean. Neatness is a characteristic of the tribe, and they are particularly dainty about their hair. Vermin is almost unknown among them, but the streets suffer from the cleanliness of the houses. All the refuse and offal are cast into the roadways, where what is not eaten by the dogs and donkeys, is allowed to fester and decay, producing an abominable stench. Most of the interior walls of the houses are whitewashed, and some are hung with brilliantly-colored blankets, and, in rare cases among the wealthier classes, with cheap calico prints. In the corners of the rooms are fire places that have a quaint, medieval look. They are usually built with a large, round hood flaring out over them from the chimney. In the evening, light is furnished by the blazing pinon wood, and they have a sort of cactus, called candle wood, which is saturated with a natural oil, and burns brightly. The houses are always owned by the women, and within them they exercise supreme authority. When a man marries, he goes to live with his wife, and all the property he possesses becomes hers.

The streets and houses of Zuni all bear a resemblance to Oriental life, and are like the teocallis of ancient Mexico, that Prescott describes in his absorbing volumes about the conquests. The graceful romanesque costumes of the women are oriental, and the bright colors they weave into their garments add a picturesque beauty to the street scenes. The monotony of the blank mud walls is broken by gaunt ladders stretching their arms sky-ward, up and down which the inhabitants clamber with agility that sailors would envy. The women and girls climb them with jars brim full of water, without spilling a drop, and the babies are able to go up and down as soon as they can walk. Even the dogs nimbly run this ladder gauntlet as easily as squirrels.

The Zunis are strictly monogamous, while the savage tribes are invariably polygamous, and as a rule the women are chaste. Adultery is severely punished, and while there is a limited amount of prostitution, those who engage in it are the outcasts of the tribe, ostracised and condemned as in civilization. The vice of Zuni is gambling, and it prevails not only there, but among all the Mexicans and Indians. It is no recent thing, but existed even in a greater degree when the Spaniards invaded the land. The old chroniclers, gazing half in admiration and half in contempt upon the amusements and customs of pueblo life, noticed particularly, and in their reports minutely described, a game which the natives played so eagerly that when they had lost all they would stake even their own bodies, and gamble themselves into slavery, as Tacitus says the old Germans used to do. According to the description, this game was one of lots, or dice, and must have been something like backgammon. Mr. Cushing describes many of their games, which are peculiar and complicated, and are worthy the study of science.

Mr. Klett, of the Wheeler Exploring Expedition, leaves on record a testimonial to the character of the Zunis. He says: "One can not but admire their regard for truth, their industry, unobtrusive disposition, hospitality, and uniform courtesy and kindness to strangers. Their hatred of the Mexicans is intensely bitter, and is not concealed. On every favorable occasion they give vent to expressions indicative of outraged feelings, by reason of the persecutions that have been inflicted upon them by their enemies; and these, with the feeling manner in which they are made known, warrant the belief that the injuries they have suffered have been numerous and severe. Their love for, and kindness toward the people of the United States (or "the Americans," as they call them,) is in striking contrast with the hatred and revenge they bear the Mexicans. Yet the benefits they have received from our government are neither many nor great. Although these Indians, like all Pueblos, do not impress the stranger favorably at first sight, on closer acquaintance he is compelled to yield to the conviction that they are among Nature's noblemen, that they are the descendants of a race long freeholders of the American continent, and are in every way worthy of confidence, admiration, and respect. Industrious and self-sustaining, they are temperate and quiet."

The Zuni children are permitted to run around the streets in a condition of almost cherubic nakedness, with seldom more clothing than a short cotton shirt; and, until they are able to walk, the babies lie as nature clothed them, except for the blanket in which they are wrapped and slung over the mother's back. The faces of all the little ones are smeared with food, and their fat little bodies are generally caked with mud, which clings to them from the pools of tepid water along the river bed, where they lie soaking during the hot hours, or scamper about splattering each other. They are as mischievous as any children are, and the poor dogs fare badly at their hands. The parents are very tender and affectionate toward their offspring, and corporal punishment is entirely unknown. The little ones are obedient and docile, and have the usual childish love for toys. Once a year there is a dance held in the plaza, for the express purpose of frightening the children and keeping them in good behavior. Characters of horrible appearance participate in the ceremonies, which are explained to be goblins who come to carry off and devour naughty boys and girls. They make the round of the village, and at their approach the parents pretend to conceal the little ones and fight off the demons, to prevent any of them being carried away. The scene is said to have a lasting effect upon their minds, and the mother has only to say that the bugbears will come, to secure obedience to maternal authority. They also have a legend of a ceremony that used to be performed, in which the worst child in the village was sacrificed to the Evil one. This is also related to the children in such a way as to promote good behavior.

Lieut. Ives describes the system of government very much as Mr. Cushing does, and was the guest of Pedro Pino, who was then Governor of the village, and is still alive. He was one of the party that visited the East in the summer of 1882. Pedro is a very old man, and was Governor of Zuni for thirty years. He was moved to tears when his party were received by President Arthur, and grasping the hand of "Washington," as they call all the Presidents, was the crowning event of his long life. When Mount Vernon was visited Pedro wept uncontrollably over the tomb of the original Washington and became sick. He explained that "while he was engaged in prayer his heart wept until his thoughts decayed," but the doctors said he caught cold on the journey down the Potomac River. While the remainder of the party went to Boston to fill their sacred reeds with water "from the Ocean of the Sunrise," the old man was compelled to remain in Washington, where he was handsomely entertained by Col. James Stevenson, of the Smithsonian Institute, and was made much of by the people. He tried very hard to adapt himself to civilized ways, and even insisted upon using a finger-bowl as well as a napkin at the table. One day his son, the present Governor, climbed the Washington Monument, and in explaining how fatiguing it was, said that he "went up and up until his thighs said no!" The old man heard the description of the view from the top of the monument with great interest, and it so excited his curiosity that he slipped out the next day, and made the attempt himself. He succeeded in reaching the top, but it exhausted him so much that he could scarcely move for the next twenty-four hours.

Lieut. Ives describes a visit he made to the ruins of Old Zuni, and says it is on a table land at the foot of which is a deep canon with a spring of water. Here, hollowed from the sandstone, was a cave, and an artificial path to it that seemed hewn out of the rocks. At various points in the ascent were barricades of stone, which the Zuni guide told him had been erected as a protection, and from which rocks had been hurled at the Spaniards at the time of Cornado's conquest. On the opposite side of the mesa (or table land) in the valley were two stone pillars, of which a curious and interesting legend was told relating to a flood, to which Nai-iu-tchi alluded in the conversation quoted on a preceding page. The legend goes that many centuries ago the waters suddenly covered the whole earth, and only those of the people who climbed to the top of the mountain were saved, the rest being swallowed by the greedy flood. As the waters kept rising the Zunis realized that the gods were angry, and intended to destroy the whole people. To appease them a sacrifice was ordered of the bravest young man and the most beautiful maiden in the village. The victims were decorated with plumes and gifts, each member of the tribe offering something, and were then cast over the precipice into the roaring torrent. The waters at once began to subside, and when the valley became dry again the young man and the maiden were found standing together, having been changed by the gods into everlasting stone, as a monument to the obedience of the Zunis and a token of promise that the floods shall never come again. It may be said that the same flood is referred to in the traditions of other tribes on the Western slope of the continent, and probably occurred several centuries before Cornado's invasion.

In his description of the ruins of Old Zuni, Lieut. Ives says that the crumbling walls were standing from two to twelve feet high, and covered several acres of ground, being surrounded by large quantities of broken pottery. The walls were built upon ruins of still greater antiquity. In one place was a large, flat rock, which appeared to have been an altar or place of sacrifice, and upon it lay many sea shells, plumes, and other ornaments, which the Indians would not permit the explorers to touch, explaining that the slightest molestation would cause the gods to be very angry and bring sorrow and trouble upon their people.

When the party were about to leave, the old Cacique took from a pouch he wore upon his breast a pinch of white powder, which he sprinkled upon the altar, and a second pinch, which he blew toward the sun, muttering prayers for the blessing of Montezuma and the sun upon his guests, as well as his own people. The powder was found to be "periole," or the flour of parched corn.

CHAPTER V.

ZUNI RELIGION AND THE PILGRIMAGE TO THE SEA.

THE Zunis are an extremely religious people. Everything they do is done under the inspiration or sanction of their gods, and they cling to their creed as tenaciously as any professor of theology in civilization. At the hazard of their lives they defended it against the military and priestly pressure of the Spaniards for 300 years. While other pueblos of Indians yielded to the force and persuasion of the armed missionaries of Rome, the Zunis successfully resisted and stand to day, as they stood in 1540, clinging to their mythical gods and worshiping the sun and the rain. There stands a church in the center of Zuni, which is now a ruin, and is used as a stable for their donkeys, that was erected, with money sent from Spain 300 years ago, by Franciscan monks, who for over two centuries endeavored to save the souls of this people; but not one of them was converted, as far as known, and early in the present century the work and the chapel were deserted, and the priests folded their vestments and carried their images away.

The Indians have a great respect for the Catholic religion, not only here, but all over the country; and in the minds of the entire savage race the same reverence exists for the cross that is found among those who better understand its significance. The Sioux and the Apaches, the two most fierce and bloody enemies the white man has met, will never disturb the telegraph, not only, as some writers have said, because of a knowledge of the mysterious current which permits the operators to tell their misdoings immediately into the ear of the great father at Washington, but because with its bar at the top the telegraph pole forms a cross.

On every road in New Mexico one will constantly see rude crosses arising from stone heaps. These crosses, according to an ancient custom, mark the places where people have died, or where some corpse has rested on its way to the burial. Every pious Mexican or Indian who passes is expected to toss a stone upon the heap, in order to protect the body from the wolves, and say a prayer for the repose of the soul.

These customs the Zuni Indian respects, but he can not be divorced from his creed, and it is useless to try to persuade him to abandon it. Even to the present day the Indians resist anything that looks like an attack upon their religion. They are particularly hostile to Mexicans, whom they regard as representatives of a religion which caused much of their blood to be shed; and when the new Indian agent for New Mexico visited them recently, they detected at once that he was a Mexican, and regarded him with suspicion. When a council was held and the agent introduced himself as the representative of the government, and told them he had come to see what he could do to improve their condition, the first question that they asked him was, "What about our religion?" The agent explained to them that they lived under a government whose laws prohibited interference with any man's religion, and that they were free to worship the gods of their fathers, but even with this assurance they were not very cordial.

There is a little mission and school north of the village, supported by a religious denomination, and a missionary resides there, but he makes little if any progress. They are as fixed in their convictions as the rocks upon which their village stands, and the only method of reaching them is to begin with the coming generation and educate the children from the cradle up.

Mr. Cushing says the teachings of Confucius are nearer the religion of the Zunis than any of the modern creeds, although they are fatalists like the Turks, and many of their ceremonials are similar to those of the ancient Egyptians and Greeks. There is a striking analogy also between their mythology and that of the old Saxons. They have many gods, but only two devils, one of them being the spirit of intelligent wickedness and cunning malice, and the other the inspirer of mistakes and blunders. They have been repeatedly described as fire-worshipers, but this is scarcely true, although they use fire a great deal, as a symbol of the sun, which is their Supreme Being, Ha-no-ona Wi-lo-na, or, as Mr. Cushing translates it, "the holder of light," and under him they have a large mythology. He is omnipotent and omniscient and reads the thoughts of men. The moon is the Mother of Women, as the sun is the Father of Men, and there is a female cacique, "the priestess of the seed," to represent her in the religious ceremonies.

Noticeable everywhere at Zuni on the housetops are chained eagles, haggard and unkempt birds, weary and miserable in confinement. They are to this people as sacred to-day as they were under the old Aztec Empire, and are worshiped here as among the children of Montezuma in the other pueblos, besides furnishing feathers for the plume sticks that are such a common feature in the religious ceremonies. These are all secret, a sort of masonry embracing the entire religion of the tribes, being divided into thirteen different branches, or societies, which, taken together, may be said to constitute the national sect or church, as well as the political system, the highest official being the cacique of the sun.

Mr. Cushing found the greatest difficulty of his whole experience in securing admission to these religious orders, but has succeeded in entering the highest class, known as the "Priesthood of the Bow," which may be compared to the 33d degree of Masonry, since members of it are admitted to the meetings of all the others, while members of the others are strictly excluded from the meetings of this. It is confined to twelve members only, who have the supreme authority in the tribe, civil as well as religious, and is the court of final appeal before which are tried all crimes that stand above the jurisdiction of the governor, who is a sort of police magistrate. There are only two crimes punishable by death, sorcery and cowardice in battle, but he who commits a murder, or even threatens it, is regarded as a wizard; and should crops fail or any misfortune come upon the tribe after the threat, or should the threatened man die, even from natural causes, he who made the assault or uttered the threat is dragged at night before the secret council of the A-pi-thlan-shi-wa-ni, or the Priesthood of the Bow, where a form of trial is gone through with, and the accused tortured into a confession or put to death. In case the latter sentence is pronounced upon him, he is secretly executed and secretly buried, none but the Priesthood knowing the manner of his death or his place of burial. Twice have men been executed since Mr. Cushing's residence in Zuni, one of them for having tried to poison his niece, and the other for murder.

At certain seasons of the year, on holy days, this highest Priesthood engages in mysterious ceremonies, which take place upon the top of the sacred Thunder Mountain, where, in the secret caves, decorated idols are set up and sacrifices made to them. Human sacrifices are not unknown in Zuni, but none have taken place since the Spanish invasion, although in their traditions references are made to such events in times of great distress. Since Mr. Cushing's admission to the Priesthood of the Bow, he has twice attended the ceremonies upon these lofty shrines, and has seen the idols placed among their predecessors of many centuries' accumulation in the secret caves. The initiation of candidates to the secret religious orders is attended with practices of the most barbarous and cruel character, the fitness of applicants being tested by their powers of endurance. In his papers for the *Century*, Mr. Cushing describes some of these occasions, although he has never told of the ordeals which he has himself experienced. Referring to them he says: "Far from blaming my foster people for these things, I look rather to the spirit of their at first imposed, but afterward voluntary sufferings, that they may place themselves beyond the evil they strive to overcome in others; may strengthen the faith of their patients in the sublime power of their medicines, given, they aver, by the gods themselves for the relief of suffering humanity. So, annually, they and their brother orders give public exhibitions of their various powers—sometimes, as is the case with the slat swallowers (or "Bearers of the Wand"), producing injuries for life, or even suffering death; but, nevertheless unflinchingly, year after year, performing their excruciating rites."

The Moquis Indians believe in the transmigration of souls, and the Zunis may have done so at some remote period. At present they believe in the immortality of the soul, and their views of a future life are a sort of mixture of Spiritualism and the doctrines of Swedenborg. The spirits of their ancestors form what may be called the body politic of the great system of gods, and are supposed to act as mediators between the powers of Heaven and the inhabitants of the earth. Their gods and the spirits of the dead have a definite place of residence at the "city of the sun" somewhere in the sky, but the latter are supposed in some vague way to inhabit the air at their will. While the party were in Boston three of Mr. Cushing's friends in that city were adopted into the tribe, two by Nai-iu-tchi and one by Lai-iu-ah-tsai-lun-k'ia. The names given them were K'ia-u-lo-ki (the Great Swallow), O-nok-thli-k'ia (the Great Dance Plume), and Thli-a-kwa (the Blue Medicine Stone, or Turquoise), all names of great honor, being those of sacred objects. The following was the prayer said by Nai-iu-tchi on the adoption of the last:

My child! this day I take you in my arms and clasp you strongly, and if it be well, then our father, the sun, will, in his road over the world, rise, reach his zenith, hold himself firmly, and smile upon you and me that our roads in life may be finished. Hence I grasp you by the hand with the hands and hearts of the gods. I add to thy wind of life that our road of life may be finished together. My child, may the light of the gods meet you! My child, *Thli-a-kwa*.

Mr. Cushing in one of his articles describes the death of a prominent member of the tribe, and the conversation he had with him as his end was approaching, which illustrates the convictions of the Zunis regarding the future life:

"To dwell with my relatives, even those whose names were wasted before my birth, is that painful to the thought?" said the old man. "Often, when we dream not, yet we see and hear them as in dreams." "A man is like a grain of corn—bury him and he molds; yet his heart lives, and springs out on the breath of life (the soul) to make him as he was, so again."

The burial of the old man is described in a most graphic manner. "Two hours after his death," writes Mr. Cushing, "the women of the same clan which had sprinkled water and meal on him when a baby, adopting him as 'their child of the sun,' bathed his body and broke a vessel of water by its side, thus renouncing all claim to him forever, and returning his being to the sun. Then four men took the blanket-roll by the corners and carried it, amid the mourning wails of the women, to the ancient burial-place. They hastily lowered it into a shallow grave, while one standing to the east said a prayer, scattered meal, food, and other offerings upon it; then they as hastily covered it over, clearing away all traces of the new-made grave. Now I know not the bone-strewn grave of 'my uncle' from those of a thousand others, for the 'silent majority' of the Zuni nation lie in the same small square. Four days later, down by the river, a little group of mourners sacrificed, with beseeching in the name of the dead, the only flowers their poor land affords—the beautiful prayer plumes of the 'birds of summerland.'"

The Zunis refer to their departed friends as "Our Lost Others," and at a council preceding the journey to the East Nai-iu-tchi repeated a beautiful tradition of the people of their tribe who went eastward "at the time when all mankind were one," and suggested perhaps that they might find traces of some of them among the Americans. At these councils all the traditions, legends, and rumors regarding the palefaces were revived and repeated over and over again. Among these was one of the first accounts that had ever been brought to Zuni concerning the whites, and it ran thus: "A strange and unknown people are the Americans, and in a far-off and unknown land they live. Thus said Our Old Ones. It is said that they are white, with short hair, and that they touch not food with their fingers, but eat with fingers and knives of iron, and talk much while eating."

After the ceremonies in the sea at Boston, the party made a trip to Salem, Mass., and as witchcraft is a capital crime in Zuni, they were very much interested in hearing the story of the energetic steps which Cotton Mather and his contemporaries took in the anti-witch crusade. One of the tribe, in making an address to the citizens on the occasion of their reception, thanked the good people of Salem for the eminent service they had done the world in exterminating the witches, and attributing to it the prosperity the whole country has since enjoyed. He told them that if they should ever be troubled with witchcraft again "not to consider their own hearts," but to put the witches to death, even if they were their dearest relations or friends.

Water is the principal object of Zuni worship, and well it may be, for it is the most precious and needful thing they have. The brightest sunshine rests upon their valleys and nestles among their canons. The earth is always covered with a generous flood of light. They have an infinite variety of landscape, and in some places a fertile soil. Nothing seems wanting for a full measure of joy but moisture, for with that the valleys would be rich and glowing with beauty and promise. But the earth is parched by drought and scorching suns, and the wind, when it rises, always carries upon its wings a heavy cargo of sand, which shifts from place to place like billows of water, destroys their gardens, and chokes up their springs.

One can scarcely find a more remarkable country; remarkable in landscape and in history. Barren hills of clay and sandstone, flung up at random out of the earth; strange jagged peaks and grotesque cliffs, yellow banks serrated by floods, and shells glistening in the billows of sand, scattered by the sea when it receded, all overhung by a rich, glowing, dreamy atmosphere, with glimpses of haze far off in the horizon, inspire a feeling of awe and wonder that a fertile country can not produce. Here is a desolate, mystic land, nothing but sunshine, burning sands, and legends, where human enterprise, in centuries that are forgotten, battled with hunger and thirst and barbarity, and where, before and since the wind swept away their trails, the silence of desolation has reigned. Everything dries here. The earth dries, the grass dries, the river dries, the wagons dry and fall to pieces. There is no juice in anything, animate or inanimate, and one listens to hear if the men and mules can walk without creaking.

The Zunis say that their gods brought them to a dry and sterile country for a home, but that their forefathers taught them the prayers and songs whereby the land might be blessed with rain. They therefore address their prayers to the spirits dwelling in the ocean, the home of all water, as the source from which their blessings come. They believe their prayers bring the clouds from the ocean, guided by the spirits of their ancestors, and the clouds give the rain. These prayers could not be efficacious, however, without the help of a drop of ocean water to start them aright.

At some unknown time in the past their fathers visited "the Ocean of the Sunset," as they call the Pacific, on a pilgrimage of adoration, and brought home with them a few pints of its water, which was guarded in their sacred reeds—as precious as a splinter from the true cross to a papist. This was almost exhausted by evaporation when Mr. Cushing proposed to them a visit to "The Land of Day," where they could re-fill their sacred vessels with water from "the Ocean of the Sunrise." The tribe was filled with joy at this suggestion.

Mr. Cushing's principal object in arranging the trip was to extend his influence in the tribe, and gain, if possible, admission to their highest secret religious order, the "Priesthood of the Bow." And he believed, also, that it would materially assist him in his researches to reveal to them the greatness of the people and the government he represented. The motives of the Indians were more interesting and complex. It was not only a religious duty they had long desired to perform, but they were anxious to see the glories of civilization. Tales of the marvelous things the Apaches and Navajos had seen on their journeys to Washington to hear the voice of the Great Father had reached the ears of the Zunis, and they considered it a great injustice and slight that representatives of their tribe had never been invited to go. "The Apaches are bad, but they have been to Washington," said the Zunis, "the Navajos are bad, and they have been also. All Indians have gone except the still-sitting ones."

At the first council of the Priesthood of the Bow, after Mr. Cushing had proposed the journey, Old Nai-ui-tchi (whom I have alluded to as a Plato in bronze), solemnly declared that as the most important reason for going, was to bring back to Zuni sacred water from the "Ocean of Sunrise," he must certainly go, as he was the custodian of the few precious drops of water from the "Ocean of the Sunset," which had been bequeathed to the tribe by their ancestors ages before.

He was the first man selected, and the remainder of the party as chosen were Pa-lo-wah-ti-wa, the governor, or political head chief of Zuni, and Mr. Cushing's brother by adoption; Lai-iu-ai-tsai-lu, or Pedro Pino, as he is commonly known, the father of Pa-lo-wah-ti-wa, and formerly governor of Zuni for thirty years, now a wrinkled old man of between eighty and ninety years; Lai-iu-ah-tsai-lun-k'ia, the priest of the temple and Mr. Cushing's father by adoption; and finally, Na-na-he, a Moqui who had been adopted into the nation by marriage.

It took a great while for them to prepare for such an arduous undertaking, and many curious ceremonies were gone through with. The start was made on the 22d of February, 1882, and religious services were held by the entire tribe in front of the Governor's residence, old Nai-ui-tchi ascending to the top of the pueblo, and blessing it with an appropriate prayer. As the little caravan moved off, the priesthood continued the services, having first prayed over every member of the party and sprinkled upon them sacred meal. When they arrived at the railway station at Wingate, they uttered a prayer of gratitude, and when the train started they opened the car windows, and praying in loud voices scattered sacred meal upon the ground. Their first astonishment was caused by the arrival of the train at Laguna, the nearest pueblo of neighbors, at the sight of which they marveled greatly, as the locomotive had taken them in four hours, a distance which it usually required them three days to make upon their fleetest ponies. They took their own food with them, and were allowed to dine in the baggage car. On the second day of the journey Nai-ui-tchi was given a ride upon the locomotive, and was quite enraptured. He regarded the iron horse with reverence and considered it a god, but was puzzled because it had to eat material food. When the fertile fields of Kansas were reached, they wondered at the great farms that lined the railroad track, and began to realize the grandeur of the country they were entering.

At Chicago they were not only interested in the attractions already referred to, but were very much astonished during a visit to the water-works, where the monstrous engines filled them with wonderment. They were anxious to touch the machinery in order that they might absorb some of its strength and influence, and were vexed with the attendants, who compelled them to remain at a safe distance. They could not leave the place, however, without going through a religious ceremony and offering prayers—not to the machinery, but to the gods who inspired genius enough in men for its construction. The lake was also a source of great joy to them, as they had never supposed there was so much water in the world as its shores embraced. When Mr. Cushing explained to them the superiority of the ocean they could scarcely believe him; but as everything had so far turned out just as he said it would, and as all the wonders he had described had been seen with their own eyes, they were willing to accept as the truth everything he said to them, although before leaving Zuni they did not consider it possible that such wonders could exist.

"It showed that the Americans are a truthful people," they said, "and not liars, like the Navajos."

They were very deferential to every one they met, and made laughable attempts at imitating the customs of civilization, considering it their duty to do honor to the Americans by adopting their manners. At Chicago they first tried American food, and the gratification was so great that they would have been gluttons but for the restraining injunctions of Mr. Cushing. At home they are a strictly temperate people, and have none of the intoxicating decoctions that other savages brew, but when wine was offered them in the East they accepted it as an American courtesy, and it pleased their palates. One of the party in explaining the influence of alcohol remarked that it "was good to the taste, but filled him with much fighting." They attempted to go through a religious ceremony at every stream they crossed, and when the railroad train hurried them over the brooks and rills of New York and New England they were kept busy with their bags of sacred meal and incessant prayers.

Mr. Cushing arranged it, upon their arrival in Boston, so that their first view of the ocean should be sudden and unexpected. The morning after they came they were taken to the tower of a lofty building without being made aware of the purpose, and when the curtains were drawn the magnificent harbor and the illimitable waters appeared suddenly before them. The Zunis stretched out their arms in adoration, breathed their silent prayers, and scattered their sacred meal toward the East. It is a view which profoundly impresses even one familiar with it, and the Indians absorbed its grandeur with mingled exultation and reverence. Their escort permitted them to feast their eyes and hearts as long as they desired, and the savages gazed silently with awe and wonder over the boundless blue waters twinkling under the brilliant sunlight. Finally Nai-iu-tchi broke the silence, exclaiming:

"It is all as Our Old Ones told us, and as I knew it would be. The blue is the ocean, and the white is the froth it throws up when it is angry."

After a week of sight-seeing it was decided to perform the ceremonies, and the Indians were taken to Deer Island, where a tent had been provided for them. Here they put on their official robes, and in the order of their rank marched out upon the beach. When they had arranged themselves in line, with their faces to the sun, their father, Nai-iu-tchi, the High Priest, blew a handful of the sacred medicine powder—the yellow pollen of flowers—upon them, uttering prayers to the water and to the sun. The sacred cigarettes and plumes (bunches of eagle feathers) of special sacrifice were borne in a sacred basket, and Nai-iu-tchi carried the ancient net-covered jar which had for centuries held the water their fathers brought from "the Ocean of the Sunset." Sacred meal was scattered about upon the beach, and the ground consecrated. Then grasping their plumesticks in their hands, and moving them up and down to keep time to the song, they joined in singing a low plaintive chant, without melody, and in the minor key, the burden of which was adoration and entreaty to the Father of Waters—the source of all moisture—the ocean. At intervals plumesticks and sacred meal were cast upon the waves. As the tide rose with every increasing wave the priests thought the coming of the waters nearer them was a token of its pleasure at their worship. Then a circle was formed upon the beach; all being seated, the sacred cigarettes were lighted, and the smoke was puffed toward the six points of the universe, to the north, south, east, and west, to the sky, and to the earth below. As the smoke rose prayers were uttered, which it was expected to bear to the gods. The feathers of the plume-sticks were invested with smoke and cast upon the sea. Then Nai-iu-tchi entered the water, filled the sacred gourds and jars, and returning to the tent another chant was sung to bless the acquired waters; prayers were said for the children of the Zunis, for the Americans, for all living men, for all living beasts, for all birds, fish, and reptiles, which concluded the ceremonies.

CHAPTER VI.

THE SEARCH FOR THE SEVEN CITIES OF GOLD.

THE first news the world had of Zuni came from the lips of a slave. His name was Tezou, and he told his master, a grandee of the court of New Spain, as Mexico was then known, that three hundred leagues to the northward lay a kingdom of seven enormous cities, known as Cibola, the land of the buffalo, which were full of gold and silver existing in virgin purity and monstrous masses; that its people knew more wealth and luxury than the courts of the old world had ever enjoyed, and that their towns were grander than those of Montezuma, which Cortez had conquered, or Peru, which Pizarro had compelled to pay tribute to the coffers of royalty and religion. He said that in these wild and mystic regions were races of highly civilized and wealthy men and beautiful women, fair as the pearls of India, and adorned with richer jewels than ever shown in the crown of the king.

The invaders of Mexico, from Cortez down, were a set of splendid marauders, so fired with chivalry, lust and religious zeal, so wildly visionary, so fanatically pious, so ambitious to conceive and so daring to execute, that they gave the history of their time the glow of romance, and the alluring tales of Tezou set their souls on fire. The Viceroy, Nuno de Guzman, organized an army of 24,000 men to overcome the kingdom of Cibola, and started over the mountains with the slave as a guide. But the difficulties were so formidable and the country was so barren that starvation stared him in the face, and, after plunging around Northern Mexico for several months, de Guzman became disheartened. The slave Tezou dying gave him a good excuse to abandon the enterprise, and he returned to the city of Mexico no wiser, and much poorer than when he left it several months before.

The subject of conquering the upper country lay in suspense for a couple of years, until the arrival at Mexico of Cabaza de Vaca after his long and weary journey over half the continent. Cabaza's experience was the most remarkable ever undergone by man. In 1528, Pamphilo de Narvaez sailed from the West Indies with a fleet of four vessels and four hundred men, for Florida, of which he had been made Governor. The vessels became separated during a storm, and that of which Cabaza was commander went to wreck somewhere on the cost of Texas, all hands being lost except the captain and three of his comrades, including Estaphan, a Moor, who played an important part in subsequent transactions. For nine years these four men wandered about the country between the Mississippi river and the Rocky mountains, searching for their companions, under the supposition that they were in Florida. They finally arrived at the old pueblo of Pecos, where they were cordially received by the natives, who had never seen the face of a white man before. The gentle savages welcomed Cabaza and his companions as the children of the sun, and brought their little ones to them in order that they might be blessed. Everywhere they found order, thrift and hospitality, and saw practiced the curious religious rites of the Aztecs. Here Cabaza learned rumors of the conquest of Mexico, and deciding to abandon the search for Florida, started southward to join his countrymen. The Indians gave them gold and silver and turquois, loaded donkeys with provisions for their use, and escorted them from pueblo to pueblo down to the valley of the Rio Grande. At last the little party reached Mexico in safety, and told their marvellous story to eager listeners who were still gloating over the hitherto uncorroborated tales of the slave.

Cabaza had gifts as a *ranconteur*, and, without realizing the consequences, gave his experience and observation a richer color than even Tezou had been able to apply. He said the cities he had visited, seven in number, were all they had been described to be, and that he had there been entertained in a manner befitting an official envoy of His Majesty the King. The people, he said, were of wondrous wealth, and boundless hospitality, that their palaces were paved with silver and lighted with jewels, and that stored away in secret vaults were untold treasures, richer than the ransom of a hundred kings; that the people were clad in a curious raiment softer than the velvet of Utrecht, that the women wore priceless gems, long ropes and chains of turquois; that the gates and pillars of their houses were of silver and gold, and studded with jewels that glistened in the sun. In them, he said, lived princes by whom he had been entertained, and that lying upon divans that were as soft as the down of angels' wings, he had been served by beautiful maidens with wine in cups of gold that weighed a pound, and with curious food borne upon platters as costly as a crown. The valleys through which he had passed glistened with jewels, and lumps of gold could be picked up in the streams as plenty as pebbles. At one point in his travels he passed over solid acres of pearls, larger than a man could carry, that glistened like a mirror in the sun. These stores of wealth were in a measure lost, he explained, because the natives did not know what use to put them to.

Most of Cabaza's story was pure fiction, told for the purpose of accentuating his really marvellous adventures, and with the expectation of gaining a royal reward for his discoveries; for as near as his trail can be traced, he only saw the mud villages of the Rio Grande Valley, and his acres of pearls must have been a bed of gypsum over which he passed. After he had rested a while at Mexico he sailed for Spain to repeat his marvels in the ears of Charles V., and lay at the feet of his royal master a few nuggets and ornaments of gold, silver and turquois, which he bore as trophies to prove the truth of what he told.

The invaders at Mexico were already suffering with a disease that nothing but conquest could cure, and Cabaza's story excited them beyond restraint. But not unmindful of his expensive failure in the former expedition, the Viceroy decided to send out a small party of explorers into the fabulous land, to continue and supplement the researches of Cabaza, under the guidance of Estaphan the Moor. The leadership of the party was assigned to a monk, named Marcos de Niza, and they started out in the summer of 1539. Traveling three hundred leagues northward de Niza came within sight of a city he called Cibola, which is clearly identified from his description as the old town of Zuni, afterward destroyed, and now a pile of ruins. Here he went into camp, set up a cross, and claimed possession of the country in the name of God and the king, under the scriptural authority that "the heathen shall be an inheritance." Estaphan was sent forward to the town with an escort of Mexican Indians, as an envoy, to parley with the natives, and see what sort of a reception the monk might expect. Arriving at Zuni the lustful Moor insolently demanded not only the wealth but the wives of its citizens, and was summarily put to death. Those who accompanied him fled back to the place where the monk was encamped, and after the sorrowful story of Estaphan's execution was related, de Niza retreated in dismay, without learning more of the country than the Indians could tell.

Upon his return to Mexico the mendacious monk covered his failure with golden lies. He reported that all Cabaza had described was strictly true; that he himself had seen the gold and jewels in the palaces of Zuni, and that his own hands had stroked the soft and feathery garments which its princes wore, but had not dared make any detailed exploration because of the turbulence Estaphan's indiscretions had created.

The ambition and avarice of the Spaniards were already inflamed by the stories of Tezou and Cabaza, and at once upon the return of de Niza an expedition was fitted out to overcome the alluring wealth and grandeur of which the old reprobate had told. An army of four hundred Spaniards and seven hundred warriors from their Aztec allies was equipped and placed under the command of a valiant soldier named Francisco Vaques de Coronado. Among his followers were many knights of noble birth and military renown, and they were all with great ceremony on Easter day sworn upon a missal containing the holy Evangels, not to abandon the enterprise until the country had been conquered for the church and the king. The next day the army took up its march, and did not return for two years.

Accompanying the expedition as secretary to its commander, and chronicler of events, was Castaneda, a literary gentleman with more regard for accuracy than the voyager Cabaza, or the Friar Marcos, and from his reports, which were written with painful detail, we learn the incidents of the journey. He describes the pitiless desert which the army entered, and the sufferings it endured, and says that when Coronado "saw there was nothing good, he could not repress his sadness, notwithstanding the marvels that were promised farther on." At the end of a fifteen days' march across the deserts of Arizona, Castaneda continues, "they came within eight leagues of Cibola, of which so much had been boasted, and it was there that the first Indians were discovered. The Indians, who knew the land, escaped easily, and not one of them was captured. On the following day, in good order, we entered the inhabited country. Cibola was the first village we discovered, and on beholding it the entire army broke forth in maledictions on Friar Marcos de Niza. God grant that he may feel more of them!"

"Cibola," writes Castaneda, "is built upon a rock, and the village is so small that in truth there are many barns in Spain that make a better appearance. The houses are built in three or four stories; they are small, not spacious, and have no courts, as a single court serves for a whole quarter. The province contains seven towns, some of which are larger and better fortified than Cibola. The Indians, ranged in good order, awaited us at some distance from the village. They were very loath to accept peace, and when they were asked to do so by our interpreters, they menaced us by gestures. Shouting our war cry of Saint Iago, we charged upon them and quickly caused them to fly. Nevertheless it was necessary to get possession of Cibola, which was no easy achievement, as the road leading to it was both narrow and winding. The general was knocked down by a blow from a stone as he mounted in the assault, and would have been slain had it not been for Garci Lopez de Cardenas and Hernandez de Alvarado, who threw themselves before him and received the blows of the stones which were intended for the commander, and fell in large numbers. As it was impossible for the inhabitants to resist the charge of the Spaniards, the village was gained in less than an hour. It was filled with provisions which were sadly needed, and in a short time the whole province was forced to accept peace."

In this way Castaneda dismisses a long chapter of cruel slaughter and malicious destruction. The towns were destroyed in the spiteful disappointment of the Spaniards at the failure to secure the plunder which their mendacious forerunners had described, and the inhabitants were driven to the cliffs and caves of the mountains.

In his report to the viceroy, which is dated from "the Province of Cibola," Aug. 3, 1540, Coronado quaintly describes his conquest and his disappointment as follows:

"It now remaineth for me to certify to your Honor of the seven cities, and of the kingdoms and the provinces whereof the Father Provincial (Niza) made report unto your Lordship, and to be brief, I can assure your Honor that he spake the truth in nothing that was reported by him, but all quite contrary, saving only the names of the cities and great houses of stone; for although they be not wrought with turquoises, or silver or gold, nor with lime or bricks, yet they are very excellent good houses, of two, three, four and five lofts high, wherein are good lodgings and fair chambers, with ladders instead of stairs, and contain cellars under the ground; and the ladders which they have for their houses are all in a manner movable and portable, which are taken away and set down where they please; and they are made of two pieces of wood and their steps as ours be. The seven cities are seven small towns, all made of the kind of houses I speak of, and they stand all within four leagues together, and they are called the kingdom of Cibola, and every one of them hath their particular name, and none of them are called Cibola, but all together they are called Cibola. In this town where I do now remain there be some two hundred houses, all compassed with walls, and I think that with the rest of the houses that are not so walled there may be five hundred. There is another town near this which is somewhat bigger than this and another of the same bigness that this is of and I send them all painted to your lordship. The people of this town seem unto me to be of reasonable stature and witty, yet they seem not to have such wit as should be."

After the ruin of Cibola, and the dispersion of its people among the mountains, Coronado commenced an exploration of the adjacent country. He sent an expedition to Moquis, and another to the Grand Canon of the Colorado, of whose wonders he learned from the Indians. While these parties were out, and the main army lay encamped in the valleys around Zuni, the knowledge of the invasion spread rapidly among the other tribes of the Territory, and there came to see Coronado a party of Indians from Cicuye (Pecos), at which Cabaza had first arrived, to offer their friendship and allegiance and treat for peace. They offered gifts of tanned skins, shields and helmets, and the General reciprocated by giving them glass beads and bells, which, as Castaneda observes, "they had never beheld before." From these emissaries the Spaniards first learned of the existence of the buffalo, and at the same time discovered that the art of tatooing was known to the Indians, as the subject was introduced by the pictures of the animal painted upon their shields, and pricked upon the arm of one of the priests.

Coronado sent Captain Hernando d' Alvarado and a party of twenty men to accompany the Indians to their home, with instructions to return in eighty days and report what he had seen. Hernando departed, and on the third day arrived at the village of Acuco, (Acoma), the inhabitants of which he reported were "the most formidable brigands in the whole province. The village," Hernando continues, "was very strongly posted, inasmuch as it was reached by only one path, and was built upon a precipice on all the other sides, at such a height that a ball from an arquebus could not reach its summit. It was entered by a stairway cut by the hand of man, which began at the bottom of a declivitous rock and led up to the village. This stairway was of suitable width for the first two hundred steps, but after these there were a hundred much more narrow, and when the top was finally to be reached it was necessary to scramble up by placing the feet in holes cut in the rock, and as the ascender could scarcely make the point of his toe enter them, he was forced to cling to the precipice with his hands. On the summit was a great arsenal of huge stones which the defenders, without exposing themselves, could roll down on the assailants, so that no army, whatever its strength might be, could force the passage. There was upon the top of the mountain a sufficient place to cultivate and store a large quantity of corn, as well as cisterns to contain water. The Indians traced lines upon the ground and forbade the Spaniards to pass over them, but seeing the latter kindly disposed they quickly sued for peace, and presented a supply of bread, deer skins, pine nuts, seeds, flour and corn."

This description applies accurately to the Acoma of the present day, which lies about fifteen miles from the track of the Atlantic & Pacific Railway, midway between Albuquerque and Fort Wingate.

Three days later Alvarado reached the province of Tiguex (Isleta) where he was kindly received on account of the Pecos guides who were known there. The captain from this point sent a letter to Coronado by an Indian runner relating what he had seen, and suggesting a removal of the camp to Tiguex which was a much better country than Zuni. In five days Cicuye (Pecos) was reached, where was found a Cacique (priest) named Bigotes, who had long mustaches, and was influential as well as noticeable on this account, because it is the practice of the

Pueblo Indians, like that of the savage tribes, to pluck the hair from their faces in youth. The Spaniards called this Cacique El Turco, because of his resemblance to the Mahomedans, and paid him a great deal of attention. From this time on El Turco became their constant companion and guide, until he suffered martydom in mistaken zeal for the welfare of his people.

According to the suggestion contained in Hernando's letter, Coronado moved his camp from Zuni to Isleta, and was there to receive the former upon his return from the upper province; being not a little pleased, so Castaneda writes, with the news he bore. The Turk, who returned with Alvarado, when he discovered the object of the invasion, told tales that surpassed those of Cabaza, and when questioned as to the existence of gold and jewels in the country, convinced Coronado that he had made a mistake in visiting Zuni, for the wondrous cities Cabaza described lay far north across a river that was two leagues wide, in a country called Quivira. Cabaza's narrations were the inventions of a man who sought the reputation of a hero and discoverer; the romances of the priest, El Turco, were intended to tempt the Spaniards to destruction. He had seen the ruin of Zuni, and had ascertained the object of the invasion to be plunder. With subtle diplomacy he gained the confidence of the invaders, and to save his people from the fate of their neighbors, sought to lead Coronado away into a desert where they should die of thirst and starvation.

As he lingered in the camp of the conquerers he drew from them the reports Cabaza and de Niza had made, and learned the story the slave Tezou had told so many years before. He revived the withered hopes of the Spaniards by solemnly asserting the truth of all these fictions, 'and they came to believe again that the sailor and the monk were not such liars after all, but that they themselves had been suffering the penalty of their own mistake in directing their invasion too far to the westward. The Turk learned from the soldiers all the knowledge they had of Florida, and the great river DeSoto had discovered (the Mississippi), and then pretended that he came from that country, and was familiar with the wonders it contained.

He told them that in the great river were fishes as large as horses, whose skins were used for tents, and whose flesh was food of the most delicious flavor; that there were canoes with twenty oarsman on either side, and that the lords of the land made long journeys in them to the sea, sitting upon a silver dias in the stern; while the prows of the boats were ornamented with eagles as large as men and made of solid gold. He declared that the commonest vessels these people used were made of sculptured silver, and that their bowls, and plates and dishes were made of gold. The Turk was believed because he spoke with great assurance, and his knowledge of metals was tested by showing him utensils of iron, copper and brass which he immediately declared were not of the same substance as those used by the inhabitants of Quivira, although bearing some resemblance in weight and color. The land where all this wealth and wonder existed lay to the northward, he said, and in May, 1541, the army took up its march, the chagrined and alarmed El Turco being impressed into service as a guide.

The good news the Turk told them wiped out the

memory of past sufferings, fatigue and disappointment, and they pressed on with enthusiasm. All this time the Pueblos had been cheerfully subsisting Coronado's army, and had received the missionary efforts of his priests with respectful consideration, but the soldiers robbed some of the Aztec temples, and the monks extinguished their sacred fires. These insults and injuries might have been patiently borne without resistance, but before commencing his journey to the unknown land, Coronado demanded of them supplies which their scanty stores were not able to furnish. Their failure to comply with his exactions brought down upon their villages fire and pillage, and the entire valley of the Rio Grande was a trail of blood and brands, as Coronado passed through it on his northward march. Several of the towns were burned and entirely destroyed, hundreds of people were slaughtered, and nearly all the cattle and sheep were seized.

From Spanish testimony, which, with the traditions of the Indians, is the only evidence we have, the peaceful occupants of the country met the invaders with a cordial greeting and a friendly hand, fed and clothed them, and received as a reward the most frightful punishment. The Spaniards, made ferocious by the greed of gold and conquest, were not satisfied with robbing them of their possessions, but raped their wives, burned their homes, and finally made them slaves. Even before the deception of the Turk was discovered, the invaders were guilty of remorseless cruelty and brutal duplicity, and while the priests who accompanied the expedition said masses for the souls of the Indians, and taught them sweet hymns of Mary and her Son, the soldiers cut their throats, butchered their wives and children, and robbed houses whose thresholds were slippery with innocent blood. The temples were pillaged, and the rude altars destroyed by the soldiers, while the priests planted the cross before the terrified people and told them the story of redeeming love. As a mixture of mad avarice, religious solicitude and frightful cruelty, the raid of Coronado stands without a parallel or a resembling incident in history. Here began the long story of fireside tragedies, of slaughter, suffering and slavery, that extends over three centuries of Spanish rule, from which the simple Pueblos were released only when the flag that represents freedom was planted in 1847 upon the so-called palace of the remorseless Dons.

The fourth day after leaving Cicuye (Pecos), the army reached what they described as a large and deep river, (probably the Cimarron), and in ten days more they came upon "tents of tanned buffalo skins, inhabited by Indians who were like Arabs, and wandered incessantly in the desert." The Indians claimed to be the owners of the immense herds of buffalo around there, and the Spaniards who had never seen the animal before were very much astonished at its size and appearance, as well as at the enormous wealth the savages had invested in such stock. In his matter of fact way, Castaneda writes of the buffalos:

"These oxen are of the bigness and color of our bulls, but their horns are not so great. They have a great bunch upon their fore-shoulders, and more hair upon their forepart than on their hinder part; and it is like wool. They have, as it were, a horse mane upon their backbone, and much hair, and very long from the knees downward. They have great tufts of hair hanging down their foreheads, and it seemeth they have beards, because of the great store of hair hanging down at their chins and throats. The males have very long tails, and a great knob or flock at the end, so that in some respects they resemble the lion, and in some other the camel. They push with their horns, they run, they overtake and kill a horse when they are in their rage and anger. Finally, it is a fierce beast of countenance and form of body. The horses fled from them, either because of their deformed shape, or else because they had never seen them. Their masters have no other riches nor substance; of them they eat, they drink, they apparel, they shoe themselves; and of their hides they made many things, as houses, shoes, apparel and ropes; of their bones they make bodkins; of their sinews and hair, thread; of their horns, maws and bladders, vessels; of their dung, fire; and of their calf skins, budgets, wherein they draw and keep water. To be short, they make so many things of them as they have need of or as may suffice them in the use of this life."

Coronado went to the Missouri River near a point south of the present location of Omaha, crossing the entire length of Kansas, but found nothing of which El Turco had told him. Says Castaneda: "The Indians of this region, so far from having large quantities of gold and silver, do not even know of such things. The Cacique wore on his breast a copper plate, of which he made a great parade, which he would not have done had he known anything about precious metals." El Turco was put to torture, and confessed that all his wonderful stories had been invented by him in order to decoy the Spaniards into the desert, where he supposed they would die of thirst and starvation, if they escaped slaughter at the hands of the Indian nomads. He explained that he had done all this as a means of ridding his people of their oppressors, but that Coronado had prevented the accomplishment of the purpose by carrying with him so many supplies, plundered from the pueblos. The man who had led this great army so far in search of destruction was by Coronado's orders strangled, and Kansas received its first baptism of martyr's blood. The indignation of the Spaniards, when they found that they had been duped, found vent in curses upon the Indians, who were afterward punished severely for El Turco's sins. Coronado went into winter quarters at Tigeux, and intended to resume his explorations in the spring, but as Castaneda relates : " Nevertheless, as often happens in the Indies, things did not turn out as people intended, but as God pleased. One day of festival the general went forth on horseback, to run at the ring with Don Pedro Maldonado, * * whose horse in springing over him kicked him in the head and placed him within two fingers of death. The result of this was, that being of a superstitious nature, and having been foretold by a certain mathematician of Salamanka that he should one day find himself omnipotent lord of a distant country, but that he should have a fall which would cause his death, he was very anxious to hasten home so as to die near his wife."

So, after a march of six thousand miles, covering a period of more than two years, and an exploration that has no parallel in history, Coronado turned his face homeward, disheartened and discouraged, the houses of gold and silver which had allured him into the desert having vanished like a dream. The returning adventurers were not cordially welcomed by the viceroy, for instead of being laden with rich booty, the haughty prince found them at his door a ragged, half famished, empty-handed band. Coronado was severely censured and deprived of his authority. He soon sailed for Spain, but received no sympathy from his royal master, and died in obscurity and disgrace, while the mendacious Cabaza had been loaded with gifts and honors as a reward for his gorgeous lies.

There is every reason to believe that Zuni was the Cibola of the Spanish fables. The description of the place in Coronado's reports and Castaneda's journal correspond, as well as its location with reference to Moquis, the grand canon of the Colorado and other points the invader visited. If it was not Zuni the place has been entirely swept away, and no traces left. There are and always will be differences of opinion upon the subject, but the great majority of antiquarians are sure that Zuni and Cibola are identical. There is an old Spanish record in the archives of the Secretary of State at Santa Fe that seems conclusive. It is the report of Captain General Don Domingo Jeronso Petriz de Cruzate, who visited Zuni in 1688, and he says clearly that it was the same place referred to by Castaneda as Cibola. This was before any question of identity was raised.

Following Coronado were priests who remained among the Indians, establishing missions and churches in the newly discovered country, making long and dangerous journeys among the barbarous nations, and their traces can be seen to-day in the ruined churches and the vestiges of the Christian faith that exist among all the tribes of the mountains and the valleys. Nothing in the pages of romance can surpass their adventures, and nothing in the history of religion can exceed their zeal.

That mendacious monk, Marcos de Niza, left an illegitimate son, who also became a friar, and in 1580, with a party of Franciscans, went to Zuni to establish a mission and convert to the true religion the Indians of whom his father had told such falsehoods. They were driven away, and one of the party murdered. This angered the Viceroy and he sent the monks back with one Don Antonio Esperjo, at the head of a party of soldiers to reason with the resisting heathen. Then was built the old church which still stands in the center of Zuni, and is used to-day as a stable for donkeys, but no *Gloria* or *Te Deum* has been sung in it for a hundred years. Intimidated by the sabers of the Spaniards the Indians accepted the religion of the self-appointed guardians of their souls, and under the direction of the monks built what was in its time, and under the circumstances, a splendid edifice. It is large enough to hold four or five hundred people, and the walls are massive. The altar timbers were handsomely carved by skillful monks, and it was decorated with handsome pictures and ornaments given to the cause of evangelization by the pious Queen of Spain. In this church the Zunis went through the forms of worship, and kneeled before a cross, the significance of which they could not appreciate, until the rebellion of 1681, when they killed their priests and threw off the religious as well as the civil yoke.

There is a tradition that the priest at Zuni saved his head by abjuring the faith and turning Indian. The story goes that when the Spaniards went there at the time of the re-conquest, about 1690, and again chased the natives into the rocks, they inquired for the padre, who called out over the barricades that he was alive and well; but being shorn of his priestly robes and wearing the Zuni costume they did not recognize him, and asked if he could write. He answered that he could, but had no pens or paper. They passed him up a piece of parchment upon which he traced a message with the end of a brand. This satisfied them of his identity, and through him they made terms with the Zunis without further slaughter. But there is no allusion to this interesting incident in the records of the time, which are otherwise complete, and the antiquarians repudiate it.

It is, however, true that although the Indians in other pueblos endeavored to obliterate every trace of their cruel rulers in this rebellion, the Catholic church at Zuni was undisturbed. The altar stood until a few years since when the most valuable pictures and carvings were borne away by relic vandals, and the timbers were used from time to time to supply the need of fire wood.

CHAPTER VII.

QUEER PEOPLE IN QUEER PLACES.

DURING Coronado's invasion he visited eight provinces, as he called them, populated by Pueblo Indians. From his descriptions and those of his comrades they can all be identified, and exist at the present day. His list, however, does not include all the pueblos, and while some may have escaped his attention, it is more probable that in the use of the word "Province" he intended to include several villages under a single name; some of which no longer exist, and others are only heaps of ruins. The places which Coronado names are Cibola (Zuni), Tusayan (Moquis), Acuco (Acoma), which probably included Laguna; Tigeux (Isleta), Quirex (San Felipe), Cicuye (Pecos), Hermez (Jemez), and Brada (Toas). When the Territory of New Mexico was ceded to the United States there were twenty-six pueblos, extending from Toas in the north to Isleta in the south, a distance of two hundred miles along the Rio Grande River, not including Moquis, which is in Arizona. These towns were Toas, Nambe, Tezuque, Pojanque, San Juan, San Yldefonzo, Santa Clara, Sandia, and Isleta, speaking one language; Pictoris, Jemez, Santo Domingo, San Felipe, Santa Anna, Cocluti, Silla, Laguna, and Acoma, speaking another, and Zuni, speaking a third. The Zunis and Moquis have entirely different languages from the remaining pueblos, and are not understood by each other; but in the pueblos of the Rio Grande the fundamental principles of the vocabularies are the same, although two dialects are spoken.

At the time of annexation the pueblo population was about 20,000, but since then it has been greatly reduced by disease, the small pox being the great exterminator. For example, in the census of 1850, as given by Schoolcraft, the Zunis numbered 2,985 people, while in the census of 1880, taken by Cushing, the total was but 1,602. This ratio of depopulation has been going on ever since the time of the Spaniards, and therefore when Coronado discovered their existence the pueblos of New Mexico must have contained two hundred thousand people or more. One nation, the Tagnos, has entirely disappeared from the face of the earth, and many of the villages, like Pecos, have nothing but memories and a few ruins to mark where once lived a populous and prosperous community. Many of these towns were destroyed during the Spanish invasion, others were razed during the several rebellions, while more have been depopulated by disease and abandoned by the survivors. The small pox, brought in by the whites, has destroyed more than war, and the filth of the villages has tempted other contagions. A well-known physician of Santa Fe observes that if it were not for the pure atmosphere epidemics would never cease.

That inordinate thirst for gold which marked the Spanish pioneer in all parts of the world was accentuated in New Mexico, and not content with stripping the natives of their property and compelling them to bow allegiance to the king, the conquerors compelled them to abandon their religion and made them slaves. Their ancient rites were prohibited and their temples destroyed; the women were debauched and the men were driven by task-masters more cruel than those of Egypt. Finally, a rebellion broke out in 1680, in which the pueblo of San Juan alone remained faithful to the Spaniards, in token whereof it has since been called *San Juan de los Caballeros*, or "San Juan of the Gentlemen." After several battles the Spaniards took refuge in Santa Fe, from which they were driven with the most bloody slaughter. The Indians gathered in the plaza, and held rejoicings in honor of their victory. Every trace of the hateful Spaniards was destroyed, their houses and their churches were sacked, and a great fire was kindled of the plunder in the plaza, in which the bodies of the dead were burned. The monument which stands there to-day in honor of the heroes of 1861 rests upon the bones of tyrants who died a century before our government was founded.

When the destruction was complete the Indians went back to their homes and resumed the life they led before their country was invaded. In 1693, however, a Spanish army from Mexico, under Diego de Vargas, recovered possession, destroying some of the pueblos, and whipping others into submission. The rebellion taught the Spaniards a lesson of humanity, and a new regime was inaugurated, in which the Catholic religion was enforced and slavery was continued, but with less barbarism, and not until 1837 was there another revolt. This time the Indians were assisted and encouraged by Mexican politicians. The head of Perez, the Governor, was kicked about the plaza of Santa Fe like a football, and the bodies of his officials were hacked and torn asunder by the maddened peons. A

Toas Indian named Jose Gonzales was made Governor, but his authority was brief, as the Mexican Government took immediate steps to crush the insurrection, and General Armijo was installed in the old, low adobe building called the *Palace del Gobernador*, and reigned there until he fled before the advance of the gallant Phil Kearney in 1847. Kearney was heralded as the redeemer which Montezuma had prophesied would come, and ever since he rescued them from slavery the Indians have worshiped him as a saint.

Toas has been better known than any of the other pueblos, as it was a trading post in early times and attracted the residence of many Mexicans. It was the headquarters and base of supplies of many of the earlier exploring expeditions, and the rich mines in the mountains around drew to it much notoriety and emigration. Kit Carson and Maxwell, his partner, lived and married there, and the old home of Fremont's guide, companion, and friend is now a boarding house.

The Indians of Taos were more influential, less scrupulous and shrewder than those of the other pueblos, and all of the rebellions originated there. The rebellion of 1680 was planned and led by a Toas native named Pope, who pretended to have the gift of supernatural powers, and convinced his simple-minded brethren that the gods had revealed to him their will that all the Spaniards be destroyed. In the rebellion of 1837 Jose Gonzales, a native and resident of Taos, was the chief conspirator. In 1847 the first Governor of New Mexico under United States authority, Colonel Bent, was assassinated at Taos in the most fiendish way.

The pueblos in the Rio Grande valley have lost much of their primitiveness by contact with the Mexicans and Americans, and to see Aztec life one has to go into the isolated villages of the mountains. About fifty miles west of Albuquerque, close to the track of the Atlantic and Pacific railroad, on the west bank of the Gallo river, is the curious old town of Laguna. It stands upon the top of an enormous rock, and is built without any particular order, the houses being small, scarcely any of them more than two stories high. The walls are of mud and the structures are in terraces, entered by ladders, but are not as comfortable as those of Zuni and some of the other pueblos. In the center of the villaga is a plaza, on one side of which is the *estufa* or Aztec temple, and on the other a curious old Catholic church, with quaint pictures and rude decorations. Service is occasionally held here by an itinerant priest, but the protestants have a firmer hold upon the people, having been represented by a missionary for nearly forty years. The Rev. Mr. Gorman, a Baptist, was the first in the field, but the Rev. John Menaul is now there.

The Lagunas are the most advanced of the Pueblo tribes, principally because of the successful labor among them of Mr. Menaul, a quiet, unassuming gentleman, who has secured their confidence, and has led them gradually away from their barbarous practices and heathenish rites. He has not attempted to convert them to Christianity, nor has he endeavored to overturn their customs of centuries, but by the force of example and kindly influence has introduced among them civilized methods, and by improving their temporal welfare is slowly drawing them toward the light. Some of them have adopted the American mode of cookery, and sleep in civilized beds. The first step toward voluntary citizenship ever taken by an Indian was made by one of the Lagunas recently in filing a pre-emption claim at the land office. Several can talk English, which they learned from the track layers of the Atlantic and Pacific railroad, who camped and worked near their town for many months.

Dr. P. G. S. Tenbroek, a surgeon of the United States army, writing of a visit to Laguna in 1852, says: " The town is forty-five miles west of Albuquerque. The people live in fixed abodes and cultivate the soil. Many of them have embraced the Catholic faith, but still retain their ancient superstition, and preserve the sacred fire of Montezuma. The town is built upon a rocky eminence near the base of which is a small lake (laguna) which supplies them with water. Their farms are in the valley to the north. The population is about 900. The houses are built of mud, and like all other pueblos consist of several stories built up in a terraced form, and as they have no doors opening upon the ground one must mount the roof by means of a ladder to gain admittance. The government consists of a Governor, elected annually by the people, who has the entire control of affairs in the pueblo, and settles all disputes. He has a council of old men called caciques. They have a kind of under ground room called the *estufa*, which is like our city halls, and is the place where all their councils, religious ceremonies and dances are held. In another place the sacred fire, which is attended by the oldest men, and never allowed to go out, is kept. They also have a war captain, who is chosen from the most distinguished braves. No man or woman is allowed to marry out of the tribe. In spinning and weaving they use a spindle and a single upright loom. The men knit their own stockings. They use mill stones similar to those employed by the Mexicans, and upon these they grind a very fine flour from corn, which is made into paste and baked upon a flat stone in sheets no thicker than letter paper. This bread is called gugave. They make earthenware, some of which is beautifully painted. Their customs are similar to those of the ancient Aztecs, from whom they are derived. This pueblo is very old as the deep worn trails in the rock testify. They have Spanish documents dating back three hundred years."

Dr. Tenbroek describes a funeral he saw at Laguna. "The grave was dug and the corpse, sewed up in a blanket, was lowered into its narrow house. When it was placed in the grave each friend of the deceased threw in a handful of earth, then the females of the family approached in a mournful procession (while the males stood around in solemn silence), each bearing on her head a *tinaja*, or water jar, filled with water, which she emptied into the grave, and whilst doing so commenced the death cry, till the sad lament, growing louder and louder, swelled through the whole place. Out of the yard they passed in Indian file, sending forth the most doleful cries, and long after I lost sight of them I could hear the plaintive moans. I never in my life heard any sound so touchingly sad and plaintive. The great men are all buried in the church, and none of their bodies are allowed to remain long in the grave, but after a certain time are disinterred, and the bones placed in storehouses built for the purpose. One of these on the east side of the church has fallen down, and discloses an immense pile of skulls and bones. They believe that on a certain day (in August I think) the dead rise from their graves and flit about among the neighboring hills, and all who have lost friends carry out quantities of bread and meat, and such other good things as they can obtain, and place them in the haunts frequented by the dead."

The Laguna Indians worship Montezuma, and have an image of the god. A traveler who visited the place in 1865 writes of seeing it. He says: "Having expressed a desire to see their god, Montezuma, my young guide led the way to the house where the famous deity is kept. This is the most cherished and probably the only one still retained of all their ancient heathen gods. It is greatly in vogue in a dry time, when it is brought forth from the sanctuary, and, with dancing and other rites they invoke it for rain. But whether it has ever been able to bring refreshing showers to the parched earth is a question open to discussion.

"We picked up one of the head men on the way, who accompanied us. We ascended a ladder and entered a small and badly lighted room, where we found a shriveled up old Indian, entirely naked except a small cloth about his loins and moccasins upon his feet. The guide made known the object of our visit and told him we were not Mexicans, and would neither injure nor carry away the god, which assurance was necessary, as none of that race are permitted to look upon it. A conference was now held between the man who accompanied us, the old keeper, and an old hag of a woman, who in the meantime had come in; and in a few minutes we were informed that we could see Montezuma. The old woman was dispatched to bring it in, who returned after a short absence carrying something in her arms wrapped up in an old cloth, which she placed carefully upon the floor. The cloth was then removed, and their favorite god stood before our eyes.

"I was much disappointed in its appearance, it being a much ruder affair than I was prepared to see. I had expected to see something in imitation of man or beast, but there was presented to our sight an object that neither resembled anything upon the earth, the heavens above, or in the sea beneath, and I felt that it could hardly be sinful in the poor ignorant Indian to worship such an object.

"The god is made of tanned skin of some sort, and the form is circular, being about nine inches in heighth, and the same in diameter. The top is covered with the same material, but the lower end is open, one half being painted red and the other green. Upon the green side is fashioned a rude representation of a man's face; two oblong aperatures in the skin in the shape of right angle triangles, with the bases inward, are the eyes. There is no nose, and a circular piece of leather fastened about two inches below the eyes represents the mouth. Two similar pieces on each side, opposite the outer corners of the eyes, are intended for the ears. This completes the personel of the god, with the addition of a small tuft of leather upon the top, which is dressed with feathers when it is brought out to be worshipped on public occasions. The three Indians present looked upon it with the greatest veneration, who knelt around it in the most devout manner, and went through a form of prayer, while one of the number sprinkled upon it a white powder. Matteo, the Indian who accompanied us, spoke in praise of Montezuma, and told us that it was god and the brother of the sun."

Twenty miles north is an ancient ruin, so old that the present Indians have no knowledge of its origin or former occupants. They only know that it was there when their fathers came. Under the ruins are excavated cellars which are not often found in the pueblos of to-day.

The town of Acoma, which lies fifteen or twenty miles north of Laguna, is one of the most ancient and remarkable in the Pueblo group, and with the exception of Moquis and Zuni, has yielded less of its ancient customs to the influence of civilization. The place stands upon the summit of an enormous rock, white, and almost perpendicular. The only way to get to it is up a path carved by human hands in the crevices of the sandstone, which is long, steep and narrow. No wheeled vehicle has ever entered the pueblo, but supplies are carried upon the backs of surefooted donkeys. There has been little if any change since Coronado came here in 1540. The careful Castaneda, the chronicler of his expedition, described Acoma as "a very strong place built upon a rock, very high and on three sides perpendicular. The only means of reaching the top is by ascending a staircase cut in the solid rock. The first flight of steps numbered two hundred, which could only be ascended with difficulty. The second flight numbered a hundred more, narrower and more difficult than the first, and when they were surmounted there remained about twelve more at the top which could only be ascended by putting the hands and feet into the holes cut in the rock."

At Acoma the same customs exist as at Zuni, and the

inhabitants of the two places are very much alike except in language. A visitor in 1871 describes a manuscript he saw there in the possession of an old cacique, which was regarded with the greatest reverence, and the people feared that some misfortune would befall them if it were touched by sacrilegious hands. It was discovered to be a very ancient missal, written upon parchment with a plain round hand. The document was probably left by the Franciscan monks, who built an adobe church there centuries ago, and until recently occupied an ancient and shattered house adjoining it. The church is a curious old structure, and is decorated with two pictures, a Virgin and Child and a St. Joseph, which are said to be of value, having been imported from Spain at least two hundred years ago. The ceiling bears a rude fresco representing the sun, moon and stars, which the Indians say was the work of an artist priest. His name and the date (1702) can be found under the dust that has been accumulating for generations. There is a pair of bells in the tower of the church, which are said to be the gift of the Queen of Spain, but the date when they were brought there cannot be ascertained.

Although the Catholics have maintained their mission here for three centuries, the people still cling to the Aztec rites, and keep the sacred fire burning in the *estufa*. It was seen several years ago by an army officer, who found four old caciques watching it, busying themselves with the weaving of blankets. The people have no doubt lost the substance of the Aztec religion, but retain this, with some of the ceremonials. They go to the house-tops each morning to watch for the coming of Montezuma, their

Messiah. As the first faint streak of red lights up the low horizon, tall dark figures appear upon the parapets of the town, and remain facing the dawn until the sun is fairly in the heavens. Then the muffled forms drop away slowly and sadly, for another morn has brought disappointment to the patient souls that have watched, oh! so long and persistently, for the arrival of their redeemer. What they expect him to do for them, what hopes they have in his bright coming, has not been clearly determined; but in their steadfast hearts there is an enduring faith which centuries of waiting have not dimmed, nor the showers of blood from Spanish sabres extinguished, that the dawn of his appearance will bring a brighter day.

The Moquis are an isolated relic of a once great nation. Their home, like Acoma, is upon a high, rocky island, separated from the rest of the world by an ocean of sand. It is a natural fortification, and can be approached only by climbing a long, narrow serpentine path in the crevices of the rocks. In Coronado's time Moquis was known as the Province of Tusayan, and consisted of seven towns with a population of about 20,000. All the villages stand to-day, but the people are reduced to a mere handful. The villages occupy the entire width of a broad mesa or table land, and standing immediately in front of the houses one may look down a precipice 500 feet. On the rim of this rocky wall the children play and the goats feed. The houses are the same as those of Zuni, except that they are built of stone instead of adobe, and the customs of the two places are similar.

Like the inhabitants of all the other pueblos, the Moquis are rapidly dwindling away, and in the thirty years during which civilization has known something of them their numbers have decreased from 6,000, according to the census of 1850, to 1,604 to-day.

The Moquis have lost some of the land they formerly occupied in the same way which the Zunis narrowly escaped losing theirs. They had cultivated cotton from time immemorial in a certain fertile valley, and when the Spaniards came here in 1540, had large fields from which they traded the surplus to other tribes. But a few years ago the Mormons, which are now swarming over Arizona, came here, pre-empted the Moquis' cotton fields, and are now actually selling cotton to the Indians from the fields which they owned and cultivated for hundreds of years.

The Moquis tradition is that their fathers used to live far in the North, and that long years ago barbarous tribes of Indians drove them from their houses into the mountains, where they now reside, and where they fortified and defended themselves. The Moquis houses are of the same order of architecture as the ruins of Colorado, their general form is identical, and the same material is used. The present villages are upon high, impregnable cliffs, while the ruins are all in the valleys. When the emigration took place cannot be determined, but it must have been centuries ago, as the houses of the present pueblos were old when the Spaniards found them in 1540, and were even then crumbling in decay. One evidence of the age of the present villages is that across the space between them paths have been worn in the solid rock to a depth of several inches, and remembering that the shoes of the people are soft-soled moccasins, the geologists think it must have been a thousand years.

Dr. Tenbroek, who visited the place in 1852, placed the population of the seven Moquis pueblos at 8,000. He says "they believe in a great father who lives where the sun rises, and a great mother who lives where the sun sets. Many, many years ago their great mother brought from her home in the west nine races of men. First, the deer race; second, the sand race; third, the water race; fourth, the bear race; fifth, the rabbit race; sixth, the wolf race; seventh, the rattlesnake race; eighth, the tobacco plant race, and ninth, the reed grass race. Having placed them here where their villages stand, she transformed them into men, who built the pueblos, and the race distinction is still kept up. One told me he was of the sand race, and another that he was of the rabbit race. The Governor is of the deer race. They are firm believers in metempsychosis, and that when they die, will resolve into their original forms and become deers, bears, etc. Shortly after the pueblos were built, the great mother came in person and brought them all the domestic animals they have, cattle, sheep and donkeys. Their sacred fire is kept burning constantly by the old men, and they fear some great misfortune would befall them if they allowed it to be extinguished.

"Their mode of marriage might be introduced into civilized life. Here, instead of the swain asking the hand of the fair one, she selects the man of her fancy and then her father proposes to the sire of the dusky youth. Polygamy is unknown among them, but if at any time husband and wife do not live happily together they are divorced and can remarry. They are a happy, simple, contented and most hospitable people. The vice of intoxication is unknown and they have no kind of fermented liquors. When a stranger visits them the first act is to set food before him and nothing is done till he has eaten. The women are the prettiest squaws I have ever seen, and are very neat and industrious. While virgins, their hair is done up on either side of the head in rolls; after marriage they wear it in braids or loosely."

Dr. Edward Palmer writes: in May, 1869, in company with the Rev. Vincent Colyer, I visited the Moquis indians. One night, while camping near the town, we wished some corn for our horses. The Governor being made aware of the fact, mounted the top of the house and called aloud. A movement was soon discernable, house-tops and doors being occupied by listeners. The Governor repeated his call several times. Soon from every quarter corn was brought in flat baskets, until more than enough was procured, for which we were expected to pay nothing, but Mr. Colyer gave them some flannel. They were surprised to see us giving corn to our horses, because it is raised with so much difficulty that they use it only for their own consumption.

"The Governors of the Moquis towns are accustomed to mount their house-tops at night and give instructions regarding the labors of the following day. The night before we left the town of Oraybi one of these harangues was made, and we were informed that the Governor had instructed all the people to go out early the next morning and kill the jack rabbits, which were eating up the corn. Early the next morning the men turned out, according to orders, accompanied by the women, whose business was to take care of the game. Rabbits are an important article of food with these Indians, and their skins are cut up into clothing. The implements used in capturing them is the boomerang, which is shied at the legs of the animals.

"The Governor invited Mr. Colyer, Lieut. Crouse and myself to dine with him at his house. He received us cordially, showing us a silver-headed ebony cane, a gift from President Lincoln. Dinner being announced, a blanket was spread upon the floor, and upon it were arranged dishes of dried peaches, a good supply of boiled mutton, and a large basket of corn cakes as blue as indigo, made from the meal of the blue corn. There were also some dishes filled with a sweet liquid made by dissolving the roasted center of the agave plant in water. There were neither plates, knives, forks, spoons or napkins, but the dinner was clean, as was everything else about the house. The bread answers for both plate and spoon. You take a piece, lay a fragment of mutton and some peaches upon it, or a little of the sweet liquid, and bolt the mass, plate, spoon and all. This dinner, though prepared and cooked by Indians, of food produced entirely by themselves, tasted better than many a meal eaten by us in the border settlements, cooked by whites."

The most interesting of all the ruined pueblos, that about which the most romance clings, is Pecos, the mythical birthplace of Montezuma,—the Nazareth of the Aztecs. It is situated on the Atchison, Topeka & Santa Fe railroad, within sight from the car windows, between the two mining camps that appear on the maps and railroad time tables as Kingman and Levy. The place was inhabited as late as 1850, but is now only a heap of ruins, having been stripped by vandals of everything except its curious legends.

General W. H. Emory, then a Lieut. of Topographical Engineers, accompanied General Kearney's army to New Mexico and California in 1846, and made the first official report of the ruins of Pecos. He says:

"Pecos, once a fortified town, is built on a promontory or rock, somewhat in the shape of a human foot. Here burned, until seven years ago, the eternal fires of Montezuma, and the remains of the architecture exhibit, in a prominent manner, the engraftment of the Catholic Church upon the ancient religion of the country. At one end of the short spur, forming the terminus of the promontory, are the remains of the "*estufa*" (temple), with all its parts distinct,—at the other are the remains of the Catholic Church, both showing the distinctive marks and emblems of the two religions. The fires from the "*estufa*" burned and sent their incense through the same altars from which was preached the doctrine of Christ. Two religions, so utterly different in theory, were here, as in all Mexico, blended in harmonious practice. The town has frequently been sacked by the Indians, but amidst the havoc of plunder the faithful priests managed to keep the fire burning in the "*estufa*," and it was continued until a few years since, when they abandoned this place and joined a tribe of the original race over the mountains, about sixty miles west. There, it is said, to this day they keep up their fire which has never been extinguished."

Gen. Fremont tells the story of Montezuma's birth. His mother was a woman of exquisite beauty, sought after and admired by all men. There came a drouth and famine in the land. Her prayers brought rain, and as the drops touched her, the fair Artemis of the Pueblos conceived.

She bore a son; a summer shower was his father, and his name was called Montezuma.

The same resemblance this myth bears to the sacred story of the Immaculate Conception, exists in the legends of Montezuma's youth, that are strangely similar to those we read in the New Testament of the days of the Child Christ. When he grew to manhood Montezuma became a prophet and priest, and one day a white eagle came and bore him away on its back. Before he left Pecos, the Pueblos say, he told them he would come again with the rising of the sun, but laid upon them the injunction to keep the sacred fire alive until his reappearance. The Spaniards came and conquered them, a harsh language was heard in their streets, and a new religion was forced upon them, but, true to their unwritten creed, the Pueblos still dream of the day when their Messiah shall descend with the dawn, crowned, plumed and anointed with the glory of Divine presence. They believe his promise is sure, and will not abandon hope till the Sun, their father, dies.

The religious faith of all the Pueblo Indians is based upon the same fundamental creed, showing a common origin; although they differ in their forms of worship, and in what may be termed the details of their theology. The difference between the creeds of the Indians in the Rio Grande valley, and those upon the mountains is marked; the former tribes having much in common, and the latter differing to a greater extent. Those in the valley believe there is but one god,—those in the mountains worship many. The former hold Montezuma as equal to God, and have a sort of trinity composed of God, Montezuma and the Sun. They address their prayers to the two latter, as the Christians do to the Father and to the Son. They address the Sun more frequently and freely because, as they say, they can see him, because he looks upon them, knows their wants and answers their prayers. The Moon is the wife of the Sun, and the Stars are their children.

The legends of the Rio Grande Pueblos are nearly all similar. The story of Montezuma exists with very little variation among them all. They agree that he was born at Pecos, and that in the flight of the eagle which carried him away wherever he stopped a Pueblo arose. Pecos is the first in order,—the farthest north of all the Pueblos, then come Taos, San Juan, Tesuque, San Domingo, San Felipe, Laguna, Acoma, Zuni, Moquis, and others in order, marking the stops which the eagle made, until it finally alighted at the base of the mountain Popocatapetl, where Montezuma built a great city which was ruled over by a long line of kings bearing his name.

At Pecos there used to be a pinon tree which was said to have been planted by Montezuma, and the old priests say that sitting under its shade he used to make his prophecies, and talk in parables, as the founder of the Christian religion did. Here he foretold, several centuries in advance of its occurrence, the Spanish invasion. He warned his people that the conquerors would come from the south, and make them slaves for 250 years, and that then a white race of mighty warriors, gifted in the arts of war and peace, riding upon snow-white chargers, would arrive from the east and rescue them; that the earth then would be fertilized by rain, that the mountains would yield up their treasures to the pale faces, and that the people would grow rich and fat with herds of cattle and sheep. This prediction, made before or after the fact, as the case may be, was strangely fulfilled in 1847, for the day after the tree fell by the force of a mighty wind, the gallant Phil Kearney came down the valley, mounted upon a magnificent white stallion, at the head of 3,000 pale faced soldiers, and tipped over the deputy throne that the Viceroy Armijo had set up at Santa Fe. The pious Pueblos believe that Kearney was their deliverer from the Spanish yoke, and every morning when they go to the house tops to look for the coming of Montezuma, they take from the buckskin pouches they wear upon their breasts a pinch of sacred powder made from the flour of parched corn, and puff it into the air, breathing a prayer for the repose of Kearney's soul, and begging a blessing from Montezuma upon the work of the day.

It is in this Oriental act that the strange anomaly in their mixed religion appears, as it does in so many other ways. The old Spanish marauders who invaded this land were pious cut-throats, and brought their priests with them when they came. At the head of the Spanish armies a cross was borne and the church militant was the church triumphant. Everywhere a garrison was left, remained Franciscan monks, who, with the aid of the soldiery, compelled the Aztecs to adopt the creed of Rome. Religion was shot into them, and the prayers of the friars arose in the smoke of battle. The invasion was a grand, bloody missionary tour, and the peaceful heathen were compelled to bow before the cross while the Spanish steel cut their hamstrings. The monks did their work thoroughly, and after a few generations every pueblo contained a church, and every time the shadow of the cross fell upon their eyes the people bowed to a symbol that represented at once the sacrifice and the triumph of the Messiah of Nazareth.

There were never more sincere or devout adherents to the church of Rome than are the people of some of the pueblos to-day, but in their piety appears that strange and pathetic contrast to which I have alluded. The priests were able to compel them to adopt a new religion, but were never able to persuade them to abandon the old. They go to the housetops at sunrise to watch for the coming of one Messiah, and then, entering their houses, drop upon their knees before the cross upon which another Messiah died. The Catholic faith was firmly and eternally engrafted upon the pre-historic religion of the Aztecs, but the old faith did not expire in the process. The sacred fires from the *estufa* send to the skies to-day, as they did five centuries ago, the incense of the pinons, but they burn upon the same altar that bears the wafers and the wine that typify the body and the blood of Christ. The two religions, essentially so far apart in theory, are perfectly blended. The cross is reverenced even as much as the memories of Montezuma, and in both trusts the ignorant, unlettered people are sincere.

CHAPTER VIII.

THE GREATEST WONDER IN THE WORLD.

THE most wonderful river in the world is on our own continent, yet it is that of which we know the least, and that which the fewest of us have seen. More citizens of the United States have crossed the Ganges and sailed upon the Amazon than have visited the Colorado of the West; and the Rhine is familiar to hundreds, yes, thousands, of Americans, who could not tell, if questioned, where the waters of the Colorado come from and whither they go. Yet no scientist who has seen all the great natural wonders of the earth will deny its canons the foremost place among them; and no artist will admit that its grandeur and beauty can be anywhere surpassed. As a single scenic picture Niagara Falls stands without rivalry; but if Niagara River from the foot of the falls to the whirlpool were extended a thousand miles, and the cliffs which enclose it were raised ten and twenty times higher; if it were more than a mile from the floor of Suspension bridge to the surface of the water, instead of a few hundred feet, the grand canons of the Colorado would be reproduced, without the grotesque shapes and gorgeous colors in which its crags and peaks are framed and painted.

In less than fifty years after the discovery of America, Spanish missionaries and explorers were traveling upon the Colorado, and along its banks, and more was known of it than of the Mississippi or the Potomac, and the Hudson River had not then been named. Before the landing of the Pilgrims its wonders were discussed in the Royal Courts of Spain, and there were boats upon it before the Bay of Boston was discovered. But for three centuries afterward white men saw and knew little of it, its gorges and cataracts forming an insurmountable barrier that obstructed its exploration. The traditions of the Zunis, that their forefathers had information of the ocean of the sunset, and frequently visited it for worship and other purposes, find a remarkable corroboration in the report of Fernando Alarcon, an officer in the Spanish navy, who set out by sea with the good ships St. Peter and St. Catherine to explore the Pacific coast at the same time Coronado began his march toward the seven cities of Cibola. Having followed up the coast of Western Mexico for a distance, he ascertained that the water in which he was sailing was a gulf (the Gulf of California), and not a strait, as was then supposed. He reached the mouth of the Rio Colorado, left his vessels there and then proceeded up the river in small boats, a distance of 290 miles, passed the mouth of the Rio Gila, where Fort Yuma is situated, and when he could go no farther by reason of the rapid current, he erected a massive cross and baptized the river "Bon Guide," in honor of the motto upon the escutcheon of Don Antonio de Mendoca, the Viceroy of New Spain. Upon the bark of a tree beside the cross he carved these words, in Spanish characters:

"Alarcon hath come thus far; there are papers at the foot of this tree."

The buried papers consisted of a copy of his log book,

descriptions of what he had seen and encountered, a roster of his party and an outline of his future plans. They were afterward found by Melchior Diaz, a Spanish captain from Sonora, who made an exploration by land northward the next year (1541). He followed up the coast of the Gulf of California to the mouth of the Rio Colorado, which he afterward named Rio del Tizon, and being unable to cross it continued northward along its right bank to the spot where Alarcon had buried his papers. This expedition was terminated by the death of Melchior, who was accidentally killed by falling upon the point of his own lance. While Alarcon was exploring the river he came across a party of Indians, who told him of the arrival of Coronado at Zuni. They were then upon their way to the ocean, and seemed familiar with the country lying between the Rio Colorado and its shore, which is now California.

Neither Alarcon or Diaz explored the canons which lay above them; this discovery was left to Captain Cardenas, an officer of Coronado's army, who was sent by the latter with a small party of men to explore the country west of Zuni. His party went first to the Moquis villages, northwest of Zuni about eighty miles. Here they were cordially welcomed, were provided with provisions and presented with gifts, for, as Castaneda, the private secretary of Coronado, and the historian of the expedition, says: "Rumors had spread among the inhabitants that Cibola had been captured by a ferocious race of people, who bestrode animals that devoured men, and the information filled them with the greatest fear and astonishment."

Moquis was called "Tusayan," and here Cardenas

secured guides for his journey, who gave him his first information of the wonderful river. After a journey of twenty days he reached its banks, and says he "found them elevated three or four leagues in the air; and some of the single rocks that were seen standing alone in the canon, and did not seem larger than a man, were discovered upon approaching nearer to be loftier than the tower of the cathedral at Seville." Several attempts were made to reach the stream at the bottom, but were unsuccessful, although some of the party succeeded in climbing down the crevices in the cliffs far enough to see the water. Cardenas gives a graphic description of the Grand Canon, and the point from which he observed it, some where near the 35th parallel, cannot be far from where the Atlantic and Pacific Railroad crosses to-day, but he certainly did not find the side canon through which parties now reach the bed of the river from Peach Springs.

The marvelous story of Cardenas, which for centuries formed the only record of this almost mythical locality, was magnified by the reports of hunters and trappers, and scouts who professed to have seen the canons, and had conversed with Indians who had lived in them. Around the camp fire of the hunter, and in the prospector's cabin, stories were related that persons who entered the gorges in boats were seized by the remorseless waters and swallowed up; that there were whirlpools in which were still revolving, in an eternal circle, the bodies and the bones of men that had drifted there years before, and that there were underground passages into which boats had passed, never to be seen again. One of the stories was that the river was lost under the rocks for several hundred miles, and another related to cataracts thousands of feet high, whose roaring waters could be heard on distant mountain summits hundreds of miles away. There were many stories current of parties wandering on the brink of the canon, vainly endeavoring to reach the waters below, and perishing with thirst at last in sight of the river which was roaring its mockery into dying ears. And there was a myth about the canons being inhabited by a race of savage white men, unlike any creatures ever seen, and were supposed to be Indians whose color had been bleached by centuries of absence from the sun.

The Indians, too, had woven the mysteries of the gorges into their religion. Major Powell tells of a legend, to the effect that long ago, there was a great and wise chief, who mourned the death of his wife, and would not be comforted until Ta-vwoats, one of the Indian gods, came to him and told him she was in a happier land, and offered to take him there that he might see for himself, if, upon his return, he would cease to mourn. The great chief promised. Then Ta-vwoats made a trail through the mountains that intervene between that beautiful land, the balmy region in the great west, and this, the desert home of the poor Nu-ma. This trail was the canon gorge of the Colorado. Through it he led him; and, when they had returned, the deity exacted from the chief a promise that he would tell no one of the joys of that land, lest, through discontent with the circumstances of this world, they should desire to go to heaven. Then he rolled a river into the gorge, a mad, raging stream that should engulf any that might attempt to enter thereby.

"More than once," says Major Powell, in the report of

his exploration, "have I been warned by the Indians not to enter this canon. They considered it disobedience to the gods and contempt for their authority, and believed that it would surely bring upon me their wrath."

In the story of his army experience on the border, published in 1859, General Randolph B. Marcy, recently Inspector General of the Army, says: "The great canon of the Colorado—that 'Colorado' which enters the head of the gulf of California—presents a canon more wonderful than any other on the globe. From vague reports this chasm is well nigh two hundred miles long, and of fabulous depth. More than three hundred years ago Coronado, in the course of his adventurous expedition, came upon it. He declares that for several days he traveled along the crest of a lofty bluff bordering the canon, which he estimated to be nine miles high. That is, pile Mount Blanc upon top of the highest peak of the Himalayas, and then cut a gorge down from the top to the level of the ocean, and it will not be within a mile as deep as this chasm."

As late as 1858, Colonel Marcy was told by Antony Lereux, for whom he vouches as "one of the most reliable and best informed guides in New Mexico," that he had once "been at a point of this canon where he estimated the walls to be three miles high—that is, equal to a gorge cut from the summit of Mount Blanc down to the level of the Mediterranean."

In 1853, Colonel Marcy proposed to the Government to explore the canon; but there was then no appropriation which could be applied to this object, and his suggestion was not acted upon.

"Imagine," says Colonel Marcy, "then, what must be

the effect of a large stream like the Colorado traversing for two hundred miles a defile, with the perpendicular walls towering five thousand feet above the bed of the river. It is impossible that it should not contribute largely to the formation of scenery surpassing in sublimity and picturesque character any other in the world. Our landscape painters would here find rare subjects for their study, and I venture to hope that the day is not far distant when some of the most enterprising of them may be induced to penetrate this new field of art in our only remaining unexplored territory.

"A consideration, however, of vastly greater financial and national importance than those alluded to above, which might, and probably would, result from a thorough exploration of this part of the river, is the development of its mineral wealth. That gold and silver abound in that region is fully established, as those metals have been found in many localities both east and west of the Colorado. Is it not, therefore, probable that the walls of this gigantic crevice will exhibit many rich deposits. Companies are formed almost daily, and large amounts of money and labor expended in sinking shafts of one, two and three hundred feet, with the confident expectation of finding mineral deposits; but here nature has opened and exposed to view a continuous shaft two hundred miles in length and five thousand feet in depth. In the one case we have a small shaft blasted out at great expense by manual labor, showing a surface of about thirty-six hundred feet, while here nature gratuitously exhibits ten thousand millions of feet extending into the very bowels of the earth.

"Is it, then, at all without the scope of rational conjecture to predict that such an immense development of the interior strata of the earth—such a huge gulch, if I may be allowed the expression, extending so great a distance through the heart of a country as rich as this in the precious metals, may yet prove to be the El Dorado which the early Spanish explorers so long and fruitlessly sought for; and who knows but that the Government might here find a source of revenue sufficient to liquidate our national debt?''

In 1850 the first attempt at an exploration was made by the United States Government. Lieut. Derby, of the army, better known as a humorous writer—John Phœnix—made a reconnoisance from the Gulf of California to ascertain to what distance it was navigable, and was able to follow its course in a small steamer for 150 miles. In the following year Captain Sitgreaves, of the army, made an exploration of its banks, and looked down into the wonderful canons Cardenas described to Coronado. In 1854 Lieut. Whipple, in command of a surveying party of Government engineers engaged in seeking a practicable railway route across the continent, followed its banks for many miles, seeking a place to cross. In 1857 Lieut. J. C. Ives started up the river from the Gulf of California in a little steamer constructed for the purpose, and went to the 35th parallel, at the foot of the Grand canon, but could go no farther. He climbed the walls, sent his steamer back to San Francisco, and returned to Washington by way of the old Santa Fe trail. In his report he says: "For 300 miles the cut edges of the table-land rise abruptly, often perpendicularly, from the water's edge, forming walls from 3,000 to 7,000 feet high. This is the Grand canon of the Colorado, the most magnificent gorge as well as the grandest geological formation of which we have any knowledge."

After Lieut. Ives' time a few exploring parties visited the canon and wrote wonderful descriptions of it in their reports, but until 1869, when Major Powell started upon the most daring and important exploration since the time of Fremont, no practical knowledge was furnished the public.

Two great rivers, the Green and the Grand, born of the snows of the Rocky mountains, twelve or fifteen thousand feet above the sea, unite near the Eastern boundary of Utah, and form what is known as the Colorado of the West. The Grand River rises at the top of Long's peak, across the continental divide from Denver; and the Green near the top of Fremont's peak in the Wind River Mountains of Wyoming. The two joining make the largest river on the Pacific slope,—a stream 2,000 miles long, draining a country 800 miles in length by 500 in width, and covering an area of more than 400,000 square miles, larger than all New England and the Middle States, with Maryland, Virginia and Kentucky added. The descent from the elevation at which it finds its source is accomplished by a series of canons cut through a succession of plateaus, which spread out from the mountains like a gigantic stairway, each step a thousand feet or so in heighth, and many miles in breadth. Prof. Newberry estimates that the wearing away of the mountains has been on such a grand scale that they are all now only half their original size.

The region through which the Colorado flows, says Major Powell, "is set with ranges of snow-clad mountains, attaining an altitude above the sea varying from 8,000 to

14,000 feet. All winter long, on its mountain-crested rim, snow falls, filling the gorges, half burying the forests, and covering the crags and peaks with a mantle woven by the winds from the waves of the sea—a mantle of snow. When the summer sun comes, this snow melts and tumbles down the mountain sides in millions of cascades. Ten million cascade brooks unite to form a hundred rivers beset with cataracts; a hundred roaring rivers unite to form the Colorado, which rolls, a mad, turbid stream into the Gulf of California." This stream has cut deeper and deeper into the ground until its bed lies between towering cliffs of rock. It once flowed upon the top of the mountain; it has burrowed its way to the bottom. These deep, narrow gorges are called canons, and for a thousand miles or more the Colorado River has cut itself such a canon through the granite and sandstone and earth, which, piled together, are called the Rocky mountains.

Major Powell took with him a party of twelve men, experienced and hardy mountaineers, and four boats, which were loaded with rations for a year, and materials for building cabins in case he should be frozen or snowed in. He had plenty of ammunition and other supplies, all of which was divided into four equal parts, and each part loaded upon one of the boats, so that there were three months provisions and all necessary supplies and equipments in each boat, in case one or more should be lost. Major Powell tells of the description given him by an old Indian of the experience of a member of his tribe in running a canon.

"The rocks," he said, holding his hands above his head, his arms vertical, and looking up between them to the sky: "the rocks h-e-a-p, h-e-a-p high; the water go hoo-woogh, hoo-woogh; water poney (boat) h-e-a-p buck; water catch 'em; no see um Injun any more; no see 'em squaw any more; no see 'em papoose any more!"

Several years before Powell went through, a man named Ashley, with several companions, attempted the passage, and went to wreck, the entire party, with the exception of Ashley and one other, being drowned. The survivors gained the top of the cliffs, and made their way to the Mormon settlement, living upon herbs and roots. At one place Major Powell nearly lost his life. In climbing to the top of the rocks he reached a ledge from which he could not return, and, having but one arm, his position was perilous in the extreme. His men observed him, and going to the top of the cliff took off their drawers and pantaloons, and tying them together were able to reach their commander, who grasping this novel rope with his one hand was drawn to the top over a chasm 2,000 feet deep.

Three of Major Powell's men deserted him, having become tired by the hardships and frightened by the dangers of the voyage. They tried to induce the Major to go back, but he refused to do so, and the remainder of his men remained with him. The deserters were murdered by the Indians before they reached the settlements, and the exploring party emerged from their rocky prison the next day.

This Grand Canon, 200 miles long and from 3,000 to 6,000 feet deep, is the work of erosion. The process by which the result was brought about is considered by the scientists under three heads: (1) Weathering; (2) transportation; (3) corrasion. By weathering is meant the decay and disintegration of the rock by the action of the temperature, the beating of the rain, and the force of the wind. This process would have been greatly delayed if the loosened material had been allowed to remain and cover the surface. Hence, transportation becomes a powerful agent in erosion, not only by exposing the disintegrating surfaces, but by mechanical wear in the act of removal. All rocks are more or less soluble in water, and impurities in the water intensify the solvent action. But it usually happens that rocks disintegrated in this way merely fall to pieces, the hard portion remaining in the shape of sand and pebbles. The transportation of this residue by the stream is what the scientists call "corrasion." In this way the bed of the stream has been widened and deepened, but the work was also facilitated by the incessant action of the water in dissolving the rocks. The mechanical wear or erosion by a stream depends largely upon its velocity—upon the force of the waters. The geologists measure the amount of energy in a given stream by the quantity of the water and the vertical distance through which it descends. The velocity of the stream would continually increase if none of its energy were consumed in friction, but very much of it is so consumed, and reappears in whirlpools and other innumerable forms of motion. It is by some of these that the work of erosion is largely done. Of the Colorado plateau, the geologists say that the erosion, which began with the first lifting of a part above the ocean, has progressed continually to the present time. The total elevation has been about 12,000 feet; only 7,000 feet remains, that being the present altitude above the level of the sea. Five thousand feet of the general surface of the country has been worn off and carried away into the ocean by the action of the waters.

The walls of these canons, according to Prof. Newberry, who partially explored them in 1857, "are formed of great masses of granite, and other volcanic rocks, with layers of highly crystalline limestone and conglomerates, which are of equal heights, and correspond exactly on either side of the river. The unavoidable inference from these facts is that the mountain ranges once crossed the bed of the river and dammed back its flow, filling the valleys with extensive lakes. These were connected by a series of cascades and rapids, which must have been of a grandeur unparalleled by Niagara, but, as Niagara is destroying itself, so have they destroyed themselves. The stupendous precipices which tower above the stream on either side are but the trophies of its unconquerable power, the remnants of the mountain barriers through which the cataract has eaten its way in the course of a million of years, and drained the great lakes of the interior."

The canons of the Colorado are now easily accessible, and will be the resort of thousands of people from whom their wonders have hitherto been shut off by insurmountable obstacles. The Utah line of the Denver and Rio Grande Railroad Company crosses the Colorado at the confluence of the Green and Grand, above which is the wonderful "Canon of Desolation," and below "the Marble Canon," which is the most beautiful and picturesque of them all. The Grand Canon is reached by the Atlantic and Pacific Railway, which crosses the Colorado River just below its mouth.

A SUMMER SCAMPER

Over "the Old Santa Fé Trail,"

and through the Gorges to Zion.

A BRIGHT AND BREEZY LITTLE BOOK BY WILLIAM E. CURTIS, MANAGING EDITOR OF THE INTER OCEAN, CHICAGO.

IT RECITES IN A MOST ENTERTAINING WAY the romance of the early settlement of the West, and the early explorations of the Rocky Mountains by Lieut. Pike, after whom Pike's Peak was named, and General John C. Fremont. **THE STORY OF KIT CARSON** is given, and stories of other famous scouts down to the time of Buffalo Bill.

THRILLING INCIDENTS OF THE INDIAN WARS on the southwestern frontiers are related, including the campaigns of Generals Sheridan and Custer, and the story of General "Sandy" Forsythe's Seven Days Siege on the Arrikaree is told in a dramatic manner.

THE OLD SANTA FE TRAIL was the largest and most remarkable road in the world, nearly 900 miles without a bridge, and rising from the sea level to an elevation of 8,000 feet. Every mile of it is covered with history, traditions and legends, and they are for the first time gathered into a volume.

THE COLORADO CHAPTERS are devoted to incidents in the early history of the State and descriptions of the wonderful gorges and mountain passes.

THE SCAMPER ENDS AT SALT LAKE CITY, where President John Taylor is visited, and the doings of the Mormon Church and incidents in its recent history since the death of Brigham Young are reviewed.

ONE OF THE MOST CHARMING BOOKS OF TRAVEL ever written, fresh and bright, and contains a great deal of valuable information conveyed in a by-the-way style of writing, that gives it a fresh flavor.

Published by the Inter-Ocean Publishing Co.

And sent postpaid to any address upon receipt of 25 cts. Booksellers and Newsdealers supplied at wholesale rates by the Inter-Ocean Publishing Company.

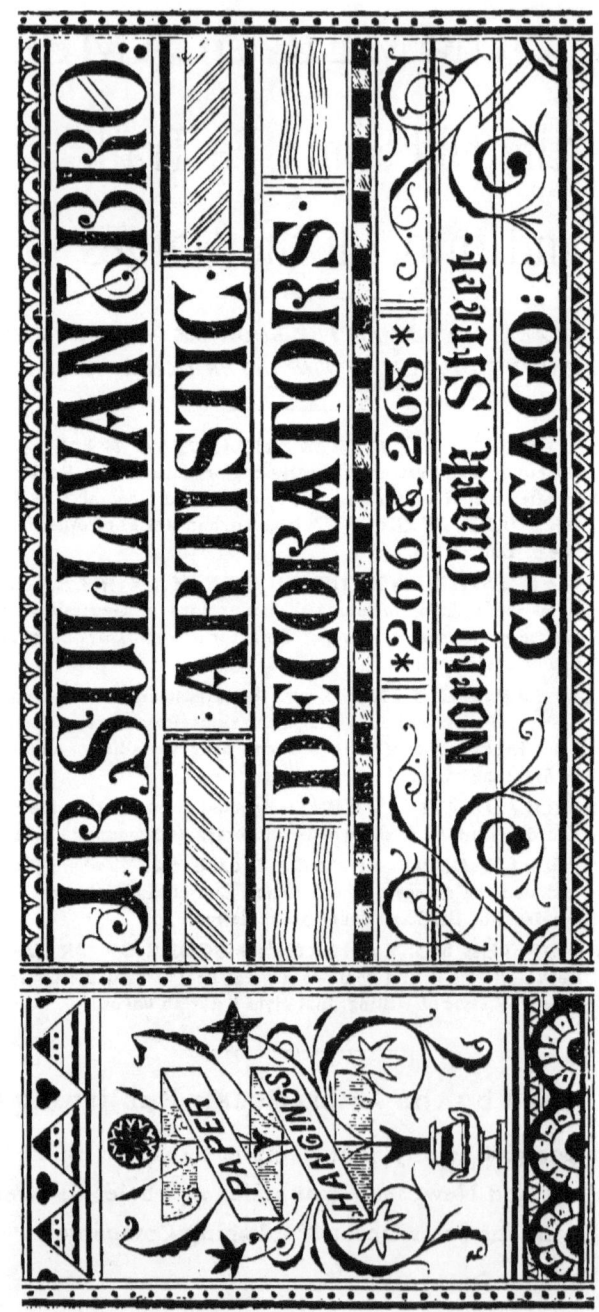

Toilet Soaps.

Perfumed with Natural Odors.

Have a Fine and Satin Finish.

Manufactured under the Supervision of the most experienced workmen.

Packets Elaborately Enveloped.

Boxes Artistically Designed.

Toilet Soaps.

"Kirk's Soaps" Marvelous in their Operation.

Use it in Cold Water. Use it in Hot Water. Use it in boiling the Clothes. Use it without boiling the Clothes. Use it as taught by long and practical experience. Use it in ANY method, old or new—in fact, in your own peculiar manner; and the result will be clean and sweet linen, wholesome in its use, giving a healthy action to the skin, and in every way conducive to health.

JAS. S. KIRK & CO., Makers of Hygienic Soaps, guarantee their goods in every particular, which are recognized in all markets as the standard of excellence for absolute purity, real worth, and genuine washing qualities.

JAS. S. KIRK & CO., CHICAGO.

"Our Curiosity Shop."

In reply to many inquiries, we are able to announce that we are now fully supplied with the volumes of

THE CURIOSITY SHOP
FOR
1880, 1881 & 1882.

The volumes are sent postpaid on receipt of price.

Bound in Paper,   -   -   -   25 Cents per Vol.
Bound in Cloth,   -   -   -   50 Cents per Vol.

All volumes before 1880 are out of print.
THE WEEKLY INTER OCEAN one year and ALL THREE of the above volumes, $1.80.
THE WEEKLY INTER OCEAN and ANY ONE of the volumes, $1.40.

HOW IT IS APPRECIATED.

IOWA CITY, Iowa, April 18, 1883.
To the Editor of THE INTER OCEAN.
Permit me, an old subscriber of the INTER OCEAN, to express my appreciation of the "Curiosity Shop," and especially of the full index. As a student the work has been of great value to me, answering at once and to the point questions political and historical which are not found in standard works, because written before the events occurred.
Please send to my address the "Curiosity Shop" for '82. Inclosed find 25c.   Very respectfully,   P. H. GRIMM.

THE WEEKLY INTER OCEAN is a large eight-page paper, [seven columns to the page], with frequent supplements, and is sent to subscribers for one dollar and fifteen cents [$1.15], payable in advance. Remittances should be made by postal order or registered letter.
Sample copies of the WEEKLY INTER OCEAN furnished on application.
THE DAILY INTER OCEAN is published every day in the year. Price, postage paid, $12.
THE SEMI-WEEKLY INTER OCEAN is published every Monday and Thursday. Price, postage paid, $2.50. Address

THE INTER OCEAN,
CHICAGO.

The Scenic Line of the World.

—THE—
Denver & Rio Grande R'y

Offers the Best Route to the

CAÑONS OF THE COLORADO

and to all points in

COLORADO,
NEW MEXICO,
UTAH AND
CALIFORNIA.

Leadville, Gunnison, Salt Lake City, Ogden, Espanola, Silverton, Colorado Springs, Manitou and Wagon Wheel Gap are local points on this line.

D. C. DODGE,
General Manager.

F. C. NIMS,
Gen'l Pass. & Ticket Agt.

MONON ROUTE

—) TO (—

Louisville and South.

ONLY line running Pullman Palace Sleeping Cars and Solid Trains from Chicago to La Fayette, Crawfordsville, Greencastle and Louisville.

THE SHORT LINE
Chicago ♠ to ♠ Indianapolis.

BEST ROUTE
TO ALL POINTS SOUTH

Office, 122 Randolph Street, - Chicago,

DEPOT, FOURTH AVE. AND POLK ST.

E. O. McCORMICK,
   Ticket Ag't, Chicago.

SIDNEY B. JONES,
   Gen'l Trav. Pass. Ag't.

MURRAY KELLER,
   Gen'l Pass. Ag't, Louisville, Ky.

www.ingramcontent.com/pod-product-compliance
Lightning Source LLC
Chambersburg PA
CBHW030255170426
43202CB00009B/749